3 Days in

HEI

Make

VISIT THE CITY

HEIDELBERG
AT A GLANCE

University

Heidelberg by Night

City Walk

The Castle

Kurpfälzisches Museum

3 Days in

Philosophers' Path

Schwetzingen Palace

Strolling and Shopping

Contents

LEGEND

⧗ Length of walk
◆ Opening times/
  departure times
▲ Transport stop
➤ see

© BKB Verlagsgesellschaft mbh
All rights reserved
8/19

Editor:
Dr. Brigitte Hintzen-Bohlen

Layout:
Andreas Ossig
BKB Verlagsgesellschaft mbh

Translation into English:
John Sykes, Cologne

Printing:
Brandt GmbH, Bonn

ISBN 978-3-940914-93-4

All contents and information
have been conscientiously
researched and carefully
checked. Nevertheless it is not
always possible to avoid errors
entirely. We are therefore
pleased to receive corrections
and proposals for additions.

BKB Verlagsgesellschaft mbh
Auerstraße 4
50733 Köln
Telephone 0221/9521460
Fax 0221/5626446
www.bkb-verlag.de
mail@bkb-verlag.de

This book is:

Welcome to

... the celebrated town on the river
Neckar which delights visitors from
all over the world with its picturesque ruined castle, historic Old
Town and beautiful surroundings.
The ancient bridge and the Print Media Academy, the old university and
the modern campus at Neuenheimer
Feld, the Church of the Holy Spirit
and Skylabs – it is the meeting of
many contrasts that keeps this city
lively and interesting. An eventful
history of more than 800 years has
left its mark on the town. The foundation of the university in 1386 was
the beginning of Heidelberg's rise to
importance beyond the immediate
region. Initially as a stronghold of
humanism, and after the Reformation as a centre of Calvinism, the
university attracted students and
researchers from far and wide.

Heidelberg ...

For many centuries prince electors resided in Heidelberg. The castle was extended to house a lavish court, and magnificent Renaissance and Baroque architecture adorned the town. After the destruction of the castle in the War of the Palatinate Succession in the late 17th century and the court's move to Mannheim, a new chapter in Heidelberg's history began following the abolition of the state of the Electoral Palatinate in 1803. The Romantic movement discovered the town, seeing the combination of lovely scenery, a picturesque ruined castle and a historic old quarter as the epitome of urban life. Their paintings and poems made the town on the river Neckar known far and wide, and it became a magnet for tourists that still attracts many

visitors today. At the same time the reorganisation of the university in 1803 laid the basis for its revival as a famous place of learning – with such success that Heidelberg enjoys worldwide recognition in the 21st century as a centre of science and research.

With its blend of small-town and international atmosphere, student environment and cosmopolitan openness, Heidelberg still fascinates visitors, inspires artists and stimulates researchers. The town also has a high quality of life. Whether you stroll along the Neckar, climb to the top of the Königstuhl, enjoy the lively and diverse cultural life in the evening or go out for entertainment, in Heidelberg you will discover a wealth of attractive options.

ised the town in paintings and poems. Today the picturesque ruined castle above the historic Old Town in the green valley of the Neckar is one of the most visited places in Germany.

● Heidelberg's location makes it one of the warmest places in Germany. On the HEILIGENBERG hill the temperature is actually about 1.5 degrees Celsius higher on average than down in the town: owing to its south-facing slope with a steep gradient of up to 45 degrees and the warming effect of down-winds, it has a remarkable micro-climate in which even almond, fig and olive trees thrive, and excellent conditions for growing grapes.

About Heidelberg

● "The city in its setting with all its surroundings has, one could say, something of the ideal ...", wrote Johann Wolfgang von Goethe in 1797. In this he anticipated what the ROMANTICS described in the 19th century when they immortal-

● The prince electors liked to drink wine, and their cellar in the castle holds the largest barrel that was ever filled with wine. The so-called GREAT BARREL has a capacity of approximately 220,000 litres and was made from the wood of about 90 oak trees from the forests of the Palatinate.

● One of Germany's oldest FUNICU-LAR RAILWAYS, opened in 1890, takes visitors up to the ruined castle. Its length of 1,020 metres from Kornmarkt up to the Königstuhl makes it one of the longest such railways in Germany.

● In Heidelberg there is also a "HEAVENLY LADDER" of some 1,600 steps that leads from Kornmarkt to the summit of the Königstuhl.

● Founded in 1386, Heidelberg UNIVERSITY is the oldest in Germany and, after the universities in Prague and Vienna, was the third-oldest in the Holy Roman Empire.

● Heidelberg's fame as a CENTRE OF SCIENCE dates back to the 19th century. Here Robert Bunsen and Gustav Robert Kirchhoff invented spectral analysis, Bunsen perfected his Bunsen burner and Hermann von Helmholtz discovered the fundamentals of hydrodynamics.

● Eleven NOBEL PRIZE-WINNERS were researchers at Heidelberg University: Philipp Lenard (Physics, 1905), Albrecht Kossel (Medicine, 1910), Otto Fritz Meyerhof (Medicine, 1922), Richard Kuhn (Chemistry, 1938), Walter Bothe (Physics, 1954), Hans Daniel Jensen (Physics, 1963), Karl Ziegler (Chemistry, 1963), Georg Wittig (Chemistry, 1979), Bert Sakmann (Medicine, 1991), Harald zur Hausen (Medicine, 2008) and Stefan Hell (Chemistry, 2014).

● Heidelberg has not only brought forth famous scientists: in 1943 Silvia Renate Sommerlath, who has been QUEEN OF SWEDEN since 1976, was born here.

● The most popular woman from Heidelberg is probably LISELOTTE, PRINCESS PALATINE, duchess of Orléans and sister-in-law to the "Sun King" Louis XIV. She wrote many thousands of letters describing court life in graphic terms. 5,000 of them have survived.

● Sunshine from Heidelberg: CAPRI-SUN! This fruit drink, 50 years old and world market leader in the segment for fruit drinks of up to 0.5 litres, is Germany's best-known juice carton, made of shining plastic and aluminium. CAPRI-SUN is produced in the little town of Eppelheim near Heidelberg.

1 Kornmarkt
2 Karlsplatz
3 Town Hall
4 Marktplatz
5 Hotel zum Ritter
6 Heiliggeistkirche
7 Alte Brücke

8 Friedrich-Ebert-
   Gedenkstätte
9 Jesuitenkirche
10 Old University /
   University Museum
11 Student Prison
12 University Library

13 Peterskirche
14 Marstallhof
   (Mensa)

M1 Café Knösel
M2 Marstall (Mensa)

Wehrsteg

Karlstor

Schloss-
garten

Schloss

Schloßstraße

Jacobsgasse

Friesenberg

Schloßberg

Am Hackteufel

Neckarmünzg.

Haupstraße

Kisselg.

Leyerg.

Obere Neckar

Heiliggeiststraße

2 Karls-
platz

Kanzleigasse

Karlstraße

Burgw.

1 Kornmarkt

Bergbahn

Kurzer
Buckel

Schloßberg

Station
Kornmarkt

Neue Schloßstraße

Neue Schloßstraße

ZIEGELHÄUSER Landstraße

NECKAR

Mönchgasse

straße

Fischerg.

3 Rathaus

Oberbadg.

4 Marktplatz

Mittelbadg.

Apothekerg.

Zwinger Straße

Unterer Fauler Pelz

Oberer Fauler Pelz

Schloßberg

7

K.-Theodor-Brücke
(Alte Brücke)

M1

6

5 Krämergasse

Floring

Haspel- gasse

Hauptstraße

Ketten- gasse

Heumannstraße

Seminarstraße

Pallas
Athene

Am Brückentor

Pfaffeng.

8

Dreikönig-
str.

Untere Straße

Heug.

9 Jesuiten-
kirche

Schulgasse

Nauenheimer Landstraße

Neckarstaden

Lauerstraße

Bussemerg.

Kleine
Mantelg.

Mantelg.

Heu-
markt

Augustinergasse

11

10 Alte
Universität

Neue
Universität

Grabengasse

12

13
Peters-
kirche

Philosophen-
gärtchen

Marstallstraße

Universitäts-
bibliothek

Sandgasse

14 Marstall-
hof

M2

Schiffgasse

Theaterstraße

Krahnen-
platz

Untere

Haupstraße

ALTSTADT

Plöck

Friedrich-Ebert-Anlage

Neckarstraße

Bauamtsgasse

Friedrichstraße

Providenz-
kirche

Bienenstraße

K.-Ludwig-Str.

Landfriedstraße

Kongresshaus
Stadthalle

Karpfengasse

Karpfengasse

März-
garten

250 m

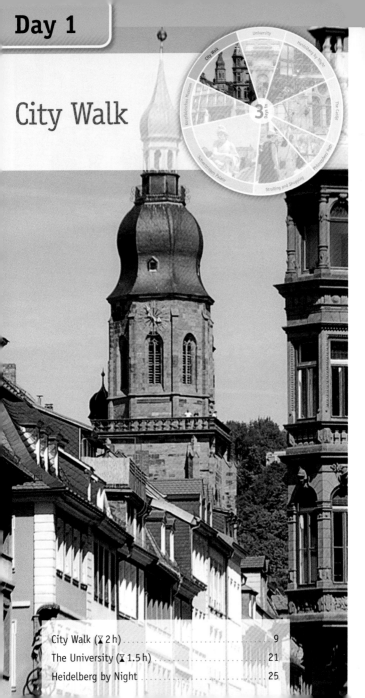

Day 1

City Walk

CHARLES DE GRAIMBERG (1774-1864)

When this French aristocrat came to the Neckar valley in 1810 to do some sketching, the castle ruin captivated him so much that he settled in Heidelberg and made its preservation his life's work. At that time it was being used only as a source of cheap stone. Graimberg rented rooms in the castle in the gatehouse tower of the Gläserner Saalbau, made and sold engravings of his Romantic views of the castle, and spent part of his fortune in restoring the buildings. Graimberg thus became the first restorer and the saviour of Heidelberg Castle! In his house on Kornmarkt he assembled a cabinet of curiosities with items that he found in the castle and the town. After his death this collection became the basis for the Kurpfälzisches Museum.

THE PEARL ON THE NECKAR – A CITY WALK

This walk through the Old Town takes you past historic buildings, along crooked alleyways and to little squares, where you will agree with Scheffel, who wrote enthusiastically: "Old Heidelberg, thou city fine, rich in honours on Neckar and Rhine, none compares with thee."

● KORNMARKT: This walk through the Old Town begins on the idyllic little square that was laid out in the 16th century on the site of the old hospital as a marketplace for milk and vegetables. It is surrounded by historic buildings such as the Palais Graimberg at the south-east corner and the *Palais Prinz Carl* on its west side. The much-visited attraction at its centre is the Kornmarkt Madonna, a Baroque statue of the Virgin Mary on a globe that is borne by putti (the original is in the Kurpfälzisches Museum). It was erected on a column in 1718 during the Counter-Reformation and was placed on the fountain at the centre of the square in 1830.

● KARLSPLATZ: From this broad square, which takes its name from Grand Duke Karl Friedrich of Baden, there is a fine view of the castle. At the centre a modern fountain commemorates the humanist and cosmographer Sebastian Münster, who began his famous work *Cosmographia* from 1521 to 1529 in the Franciscan monastery which once stood here. To the south the square is bounded by the Baroque *Grand Ducal Palace*, now the seat of the Heidelberg Academy of Sciences. The *Palais Boisserée* opposite, in which the Boisserée brothers once exhibited their art collection, now held by the Alte Pinakothek in Munich, is home to the Germanisches Institut. A few paces further on you reach the well-known historic student pubs *Zum Seppl* (1704) and *Zum Roten Ochsen* (1724), where generations of student fraternities have held their celebrations.

● MARKTPLATZ:

The market-
place is
the main
square
of the
Old Town.
When the
sun shines there
is a Mediterranean

atmosphere here. The numerous pubs and cafés put out their tables and chairs, inviting passers-by to stop for a while. This is a wonderful spot for admiring the historic buildings round about. The Baroque Rathaus (town hall) stands on the east side, the coat of arms of the prince electors above its large balcony. Take a look at the adjoining building with a turret and glockenspiel, which plays songs such as *Old Heidelberg*. At the corner of Apothekergasse stands a conspicuous Baroque building with the colourful coat of arms of the prince electors. This was once the court apothecary's shop, which had the exclusive right to supply medicine to the prince elector's court.

MEMBERS, FOXES AND OLD GENTLEMEN

In historic student drinking dens, yellowing photos, lithographs, drinking horns and other trophies serve as reminders of the merry life of student corps. These fraternities were founded in the 19th century by students who were engaged in the struggle for national unification of Germany, and today membership is regarded as an admission ticket to a position in society and business. Those "foxes" who successfully pass through the probation period to become members remain in the association all their lives. The support that they receive from the fraternity during their time as a student is then repaid once they have entered professional life and attain the status of *Alter Herr* (Old Gentleman – or Old Lady). To this day there are more than 30 fraternities in Heidelberg with over 800 students, who on official occasions usually wear colours, consisting of a student cap known as a *Couleur* and a ribbon in the colours of the corps. In the more traditional fraternities the practice of academic fencing with sharp blades, called *Mensur*, is still part of the communal life.

KARLSTOR

The eastern end of the main street, Hauptstraße, is marked by a triumphal arch that the citizens of Heidelberg erected to honour Prince Elector Karl Theodor. This classical work in the Roman tradition, built between 1775 and

1781 to plans by Nicolas de Pigage, is crowned by four Palatinate lions. On the city side, portraits of the elector and his wife decorate the Karlstor, and on its outer façade arriving visitors can read a dedicatory inscription beneath the coat of arms of the Electoral Palatinate, flanked by two lions.

● HOTEL ZUM RITTER: One of the finest buildings is the inn opposite the Heiliggeistkirche, the only one – according to the inscription on the gable, "Persta invicta, Venus" (Remain always undefeated, o beauty) – to have survived all the wars and fires in Heidelberg. Built in 1592 by the wealthy Huguenot cloth dealer Charles Bélier as a six-storey residence, for over 300 years it has been an inn. The Ritter (knight) who gave the building its name is Saint George, who can be seen up on the gable. The impressive Renaissance façade of ashlar masonry is adorned with fluted columns, beautifully carved window frames and a wealth of ornamentation.

Hauptstraße 178, www.hotel-ritter-heidelberg.com

● HEILIGGEISTKIRCHE: The Church of the Holy Spirit, a Gothic hall church with a Baroque roof and tower-top, dominates the Marktplatz. Constructed in 1398 as a burial church for the prince electors of the Palatinate, it has had an eventful history. Sometimes Catholic, sometimes Protestant, after the War of the Palatinate Succession it was even a place of worship for both confessions, who held their services in the choir and nave of the church, divided by a wall. This situation, commemorated by a plaque in the right-hand aisle on the steps to the choir, explains why there are exits on both sides. Since 1936 the church has been used by the Lutheran congregation.

The proportions of the interior, with its extremely wide aisles, are unusual. The reason is that the galleries were used in the Middle

Ages as a lecture hall for the university and also housed, among other things, a famous library, the Biblioteca Palatina. The only item among the once-magnificent furnishings and the tombs of the prince electors to have survived iconoclasm and destruction is the grave slab of Elector Ruprecht III, builder of the castle, and his wife Elisabeth von Hohenzollern, which bears royal insignia. In the nave note the 15th-century ceiling painting of a concert of angels – though the bassoon was added by a restorer in the 1950s!

In good weather do not fail to climb the 200 steps to the top of the tower, for which a wonderful view of the ruined castle and the Neckar valley is the reward.

The stalls around the nave of the church are a relic of the Middle Ages. Originally religious articles such as rosaries and saints' images were sold in these booths, but later bread and meat were sold there, and craftsmen set up shop too. A reminiscence of this are the pretzels carved in the sandstone, which served for making comparisons with the size of those that were actually sold.

◆ Mon-Sat 11am-5pm, Sun 12.30-5pm
www.ekihd.de

BIBLIOTHECA PALATINA

The Lorsch Gospels, the Codex Manesse, the Falconry Book of Emperor Frederick II and the Ottheinrich Bible are just a few of the treasures that once belonged to the Bibliotheca Palatina. The "mother of all libraries" was created in the reign of the book-loving Elector Ottheinrich (reigned 1556-59) by amalgamating the collections of the university, the collegiate library of the Heiliggeistkirche and the library of the elector's palace. However, as the university was Protestant, the library was regarded by Catholics as a hotbed of heresy, and after the conquest of Heidelberg by the forces of the Catholic League in 1622 the holdings of 3,500 manuscripts and 12,000 books and prints were taken to Rome as a gift to the papacy. Some manuscripts were

returned to Heidelberg after the Congress of Vienna, but most of them remain to this day in the Biblioteca Apostolica Vaticana.

3 Days In **TIP** Treat your soul to a ten-minute break and relax to the music that is played every weekday in the lunch-time service of the Heiliggeistkirche between 12.30 and 12.40 pm.

THE BRIDGE MONKEY

There is always a crowd of people around the modern figure of a monkey next to the bridge tower. It is a great motif for photos, and it is possible to put your head inside that of the monkey. The figure is also said to possess magic powers: if you stroke the extended finger on its right paw, you will certainly return to Heidelberg, and if you stroke its rear, you will be

prosperous. The historic function of the monkey was different. Originally placed on the bridge tower on the opposite side of the town, it displayed its naked backside to people who arrived and thus demonstrated that the authority of the bishops of Mainz ended at that point.

● ALTE BRÜCKE (KARL-THEODOR-BRÜCKE): Walk along Steingasse to the Old Bridge, which was described in enthusiastic terms by Goethe, Hölderlin and many others, and is a favourite place to meet to this day. It is named after Elector Karl Theodor, who built a stone bridge consisting of barrel vaults of red sandstone in 1786–88 to replace its wooden predecessor. The fact that the bridge was once fortified is shown on the town side by the surviving gateway flanked by twin towers, where the warden of the bridge once lived.

To express their thanks for this first stone bridge, the people of Heidelberg erected a monument to their ruler, showing the prince elector surrounded by the gods of the main rivers of the Palatinate. On the Neuenheim side of the bridge a statue of Pallas Athene, with four allegorical figures at her feet symbolising justice, piety, agriculture and trade, is a reference to the elector's government of his land, as are the representations of the arts and sciences in the reliefs of the base with cherubs. The statue of Saint John Nepomuk was taken from the previous bridge. In the Palatinate, which had just become a Catholic state, this was a deliberate symbol of the Counter-Reformation. When the statue fell into the river during the floods of 1784 it was not returned to the bridge but placed close to it on the river bank.

● REICHSPRÄSIDENT-FRIEDRICH-EBERT-GEDENKSTIFTUNG: Now walk past the little houses of the Old Town through Haspelgasse and Untere Straße to the birthplace of the first democratically elected German head of state, Friedrich Ebert (1871–1925). Here you can get a good impression of the living conditions of a family of artisans in the late 19th century. Eight persons lived without electricity and running water on an area of 46 square metres, which served during the day as a workshop for the father, a tailor.

A permanent exhibition, which is also housed in the adjoining buildings, gives information about the life and times of Friedrich Ebert. Many original documents, photos and other items reflect the history of the workers' movement and German political history between the imperial period and the Weimar Republic.

Pfaffengasse 18
♦ *Mon-Fri 9am-6pm, Sat-Sun 10am-6pm*
www.ebert-gedenkstaette.de

Have a break

If only to try a "student kiss" (➤ p. 66) you should definitely make a stop at the old-established **Café Knösel**. *Haspelgasse 20* ♦ *10am-8pm (Jan.-Mar.), 8.30am-10pm (Apr.-Dec.)*

FRIEDRICH EBERT (1871-1925)

He is one of many famous people who were laid to rest in the Bergfriedhof cemetery (➤ p. 59). Born in Heidelberg in 1871, the seventh of nine children of the tailor Karl Ebert, he was apprenticed to a saddler after leaving school. An active trade unionist, he moved with his family to Bremen, where he was elected to the city parliament and became workers' secretary of the labor union. After

election to the central committee of the SPD he moved to Berlin in 1905, was a member of the Reichstag from 1912 and one of the three chairmen of the SPD parliamentary party there from 1916. After the November Revolution Ebert became president of the Weimar Republic on 11 February 1919. As the first democratically elected head of state, he was a pioneer of German parliamentary democracy.

HEIDELBERGER HERBST

On the last Saturday in September the Old Town (Altstadt) of Heidelberg is transformed into one big festival, at which craft workers set up their stalls along the Hauptstraße, a flea market spreads through the little alley-ways, and the stands on the banks of the Neckar tempt people to stroll by and taste regional specialities. All of this is complemented by a big programme of music and theatre that is held from midday on large and small stages on the various squares of the

town. The festival also caters to younger visitors with a children's flea market and special programme for families.

www.heidelberg-marketing.de

● JESUITENKIRCHE: The Catholic counterpart to the Church of the Holy Spirit is the aisled hall church in the former Jesuit quarter of the Old Town. Construction started in the early 18th century and lasted about 150 years. It was intended that the Jesuits, who came to Heidelberg in 1622 during the Thirty Years' War and worked in the university or as school teachers and in parochial care, would promote the Counter-Reformation by supporting the Catholic prince electors. Thus the richly decorated main façade of the church with its statues of Ignatius Loyola, the founder of the Jesuit order, on the left, and of Saint Francis Xavier on the right, was modelled on the Jesuit mother church, Il Gesu in Rome. Nothing remains of the Baroque fittings inside, but the entirely white interior with gilded capitals and altars adorned with frescoes is an attractive sight.

To find out more about the work of the Jesuits in the Electoral Palatinate, visit the *Museum für sakrale Kunst und Liturgie* (Museum of Religious Art and Liturgy) in the church, which also displays saints' images, chalices and monstrances, priests' robes and a large silver Madonna by J. Ignaz Saller dating from 1736.

Merianstraße 2 ◆ Church 10am-6pm; Museum Tue-Sat 10am-5pm, Sun noon-5pm (Jun-Oct), Sat 10am-5pm, Sun noon-5pm (Nov-May), www.stadtkirche-heidelberg.de

3 TIP   To take some time out, go through the left-hand side entrance to the *Meditation Garden* of the Jesuit Church. Here, away from the bustle of the pedestrian zone, you can watch bees collecting nectar or simply admire the numerous plants and flowers.

The University

UNIVERSITÄTS-
BIBLIOTHEK.

THE UNIVERSITY STORY

When Count Palatinate and Prince Elector Ruprecht I founded Heidelberg University in 1386 with the permission of Pope Urban VI, it was the third university in the Holy Roman Empire and the first in what is today Germany, and had four faculties: theology, law, medicine and philosophy.

The university had its first age of greatness in the second half of the 16th century, when Elector Ottheinrich made it into a Protestant place of learning for his state. It became a European centre of science and culture, gaining a reputation as a stronghold of Calvinism, to which the Heidelberg Catechism in Protestant churches is testimony to this day.

SEMPER APERTUS – THE UNIVERSITY

In Germany's oldest university you can immerse yourself in the world of science and research, get to know places of learning, see old prison cells and the new dining hall, and begin to understand how a living tradition arose in the course of centuries.

● ALTE UNIVERSITÄT: The tour of various university sites begins at Universitätsplatz in the middle of the pedestrian zone. The square where students now gather around a fountain with the lion of the Palatinate was once the site of the Augustinian monastery, the largest and wealthiest in the town, where the first lectures were held and Martin Luther presented his theses in 1518. After French forces destroyed the old university complex in 1693, a new main building was constructed on the north side of the square, known as the Alte Universität (Old University). Its motto "Semper

apertus" (meaning that the book of knowledge should always be open) is to be seen in big letters in the foyer.

● UNIVERSITÄTSMUSEUM: The three rooms of the university museum on the ground floor offer a good overview of the 600-year history of the university. Exhibits, portraits and documents bear witness to the spirit of past times, and special exhibitions present a wider view of the activities of the university.

● AULA: Don't miss the room in which lectures and disputations were held. Newly fitted out in 1886 for the 500th anniversary of the university in Italian Renaissance style with magnificent wood panelling and paintings, the Aula is an impressive original location of university life. The end wall was designed as a triumphal arch with a bust of Grand Duke Friedrich of Baden, ruler of the Palatinate at that time and also rector of the university, at its centre. On either side of it two portraits can be seen: on the left Prince Elector Ruprecht I, founder of the university, on the right Margrave Karl Friedrich of Baden, who reorganised the university in 1803. Above it Pallas Athene enters Heidelberg with her retinue – rectors, researchers and the bishop of Worms, all of them persons who were active at the university over the centuries – to symbolise the entrance of wisdom with the foundation of the university. On the ceiling representations of the four original faculties – theology, jurisprudence, medicine and philosophy – can be admired. The name plates on the seats are a reference to the great numbers of renowned researchers and professors who worked here.

Grabengasse 1
◆ *Tue-Sun 10am-6pm (Apr-Oct),*
Tue-Sat 10am-4pm (Nov-Mar)
www.uni-heidelberg.de

THE UNIVERSITY STORY

Following reorganisation in 1803 by the first Grand Duke of Baden, Karl Friedrich, after which the university was named Ruperto Carola, a second period of renown began. Heidelberg was widely seen as a university for lawyers, and the collaboration of Robert Bunsen, Hermann Helmholtz, Gustav Kirchhoff and Max Weber led to a golden age in the natural sciences, which became the fifth faculty in 1891. The third great period began in the 21st century. With more than 30,000 students, the Ruperto Carola University at its three sites in the Old Town (humanities and social sciences), Bergheim (sociology, political and economic sciences) and Neuenheimer Feld (natural sciences, medicine) has an excellent reputation for research, was successful in the German "Excellence Initiative" for universities and occupies a leading position in internationally acknowledged rankings.

● STUDENT PRISON: For another sight that makes a strong impression, go to the rear side of the Alte Universität to see the cells (Karzer) in which students were imprisoned between 1778 and 1914. As the university exercised its own judicial rights at that time, it could place students under arrest for up to four weeks for minor offences such as fencing too violently, disturbing the peace at night and unruly behaviour. While serving the sentence, the students were obliged to attend lectures, but spent the rest of the time in the Karzer. This was a severe punishment in the early decades, as the prisoners were given only bread and water and slept on straw on the cold floor. From about 1900 the rules were relaxed and visitors permitted. The students then used the Karzer as a meeting place for making merry and playing cards. It gradually became fashionable for them to spend a few days in the prison at least once during their time as a student. The fates of those who were incarcerated here can be seen in thousands of graffiti that cover all the walls.

Augustinergasse 2
◆ *10am-6pm (Apr-Oct),*
Mon-Sat 10am-4pm (Nov-Mar)
www.uni-heidelberg.de

● CITY OF SCIENCE: Heidelberg has a top position for science, as its university is not only the oldest in Germany but also one of the best. This is demonstrated by the high number of patent registrations and eleven Nobel Prizes that have been awarded to professors at Heidelberg University. Several other institutions of higher education are based here, among them a school of Jewish Studies, a school of church music, a teachers' college, the SRH Hochschule and the Schiller International University. Renowned

science and research institutes such as the German Cancer Research Center, the European Laboratory for Molecular Biology, four Max Planck Institutes, the Academy of Sciences and Humanities and the Heidelberg Institute for Theoretical Studies are based in Heidelberg.

● UNIVERSITY LIBRARY: Walk past the Neue Universität, built in 1930–31 integrating the Witches' Tower of the medieval city wall, to reach what must be the university's finest building. Constructed with four wings in 1905 with numerous oriels, turrets, gables and sculptures, the Universitätsbibliothek (University Library) combines elements of German Mannerism of the late 16th century with Art Nouveau motifs. Two figures on the main entrance – on the left Prometheus, on the right a female figure with a child symbolising the passing on of knowledge from generation to generation – frame the way to the interior, where busts of famous scholars can be seen in the staircase. Glance inside the lovely green courtyard, an idyllic spot for a rest. The university library, which has over 3 million books and 1.5 million loans each year, is one

of Germany's leading libraries, and the building is always a busy place. The special attraction for visitors, in addition to many medieval treasures, donations and bequests by prince electors and professors, and interesting exhibitions, is the Codex Manesse, a world-famous medieval book of songs on 426 leaves of parchment, inscribed on both sides. It is kept in the reading room for manuscripts, the *Handschriftenlesesaal*.

Plöck 107-109, ◆ *8.30-1am, Handschriftenlesesaal Mon-Thu 8.30am-5pm, Fri 8.30am-3.30pm www.ub.uni-heidelberg.de*

GERMAN CANCER RESEARCH CENTER

As more than 500,000 people fall ill with cancer each year in Germany, in 1964 the German Cancer Research Center (Deutsche Krebsforschungszentrum, DKFZ) was founded as a national research institute. Today some 2900

people in more than 70 departments research the causes of cancer and the factors that influence the risk of contracting it. On this basis they develop new approaches for the prevention, diagnosis and therapy of cancer. The importance of this institution is shown by the award of the Nobel Prize for Medicine in 2008 to Professor Harald zur Hausen for his discovery that cancer of the cervix is caused by a virus. In collaboration with the university, the DKFZ is responsible for the National Center for Tumor Illnesses (NCT), which unites care for patients with cancer research and prevention in one organisation.

www.dkfz.de

ARCHAEOLOGICAL TEACHING COLLECTION

The plaster casts of ancient sculptures in the Marstallhof can be seen through the panes of glass. Via the Horse Tamers of Monte Cavallo you go to the *Abguss-Sammlung* (Cast Collection), which provides an illuminating survey

of the development of Greek sculpture from its beginnings until the Roman imperial period – not only for students. To view originals, go to the *Antikenmuseum* on the top floor, where painted ceramics, terracotta works, coins and bronze jewellery from ancient Mediterranean civilisations are on display.

Neues Kollegiengebäude,
Marstallhof 4
◆ *Antikenmuseum and*
Abguss-Sammlung
closed until 2022
www.klassische-
archaeologie.uni-hd.de

● PETERSKIRCHE: Opposite the library is St Peter's Church, the oldest in the town, a place of burial for scholars. In the late 19th century it was rebuilt in Gothic Revival style as a hall church with aisles and adorned with monumental paintings such as two pictures of Christ by Hans Thoma and the Sermon on the Mount by Fritz Mackensen on the north gallery. Today its artistic treasures include nine modern stained-glass windows by Johannes Schreiter.

Plöck 70 ◆ 11am-5pm (Apr-Oct), Sun 11am-2pm
www.peterskirche-heidelberg.de

● MARSTALL: To conclude the tour we go towards the banks of the Neckar to the so-called Marstall, which served as an arsenal for the castle and was defended by corner towers because it was situated outside the town walls. The name of the building refers to the use of the now-destroyed south wing for stables, with accommodation on the upper floor above them. Today this late medieval complex, which has been altered many times, houses the student dining hall, the Mensa. It is worth taking a look at the rubblestone building with a Baroque semi-hipped roof. This was the municipal tithe barn, in which hay for the horses of the Marstall was stored until 1824. It is now used for lectures.

Have a break

Visitors too find the students' Mensa a pleasant spot, either in the green courtyard or in the **Marstall** building itself!
Marstallhof 3 ◆ Mon-Sat 11am-10pm

Heidelberg by Night

TECHNOLOGIEPARK

The concentration of institutions of higher education, science and research in Heidelberg makes the town a sought-after location for companies associated with research. The Technologiepark effectively supports the innovations that arise from the co-operation of companies with educational and research institutions. It is no coincidence that Heidelberg is now one of the leading places for biotechnology both in Germany and worldwide. Since it was founded in 1984 at Neuenheimer Feld, the Technologiepark has had to be enlarged constantly. Its five sites now make an area of 80,000 square metres available. Thanks to its mix of biotechnology, medical technology, organic electronics, and information and communication technology, it has become a major provider of impulses for science and the economy.

www.technologiepark-heidelberg.de
www.dkfz.de

OUT ON THE TOWN – HEIDELBERG BY NIGHT

Heidelberg's nightlife has a lot to offer. Whether you want culture or dancing, a student pub or a cool bar, this university town has the right locations for everyone.

Plenty of alternatives are available if you plan to enjoy a cultural evening. With its five departments – opera, concerts, drama, dance and youth theatre – the *Theater und Orchester Heidelberg* alone offers a wide choice. Small private theatres such as the *Taeter-Theater* and the *Zimmertheater* are also firmly established on the cultural scene. Concerts given by the *Collegium Musicum* and the *Sinfonieorchester TonArt* enrich the musical programme, and jazz fans are catered for down in the vaults of the *Jazzhaus*. For cinema lovers in particular, Heidelberg is a delight, as a number of ambitious art-house cinemas find interested audiences in university circles (➤ p. 60 ff.).

3 **TIP** If you want to know what is going on in Heidelberg, take a look at the listings in: *www.stadtleben.de/heidelberg/kalender/* or *www.heidelberg-marketing.de.*

If you would rather go dancing, then head for the Old Town, where you will find the hotspots of Heidelberg's nightlife around the marketplace in the streets *Untere Straße* and *Steingasse*. Here is a concentration of little cocktail bars, pleasant cafés and pubs in a small area, and the atmosphere on warm summer nights is reminiscent of southern Europe. When the first rays of sun appear, tables and chairs are placed outdoors, and the life of the town takes place in the narrow

THE RIVER NECKAR

In good weather you should not miss a boat trip through the Neckartal-Odenwald Natural Park, either along the Burgenstraße (Castle Road) or downstream to the biggest industrial region on the river Rhine. Today, on its way to the Rhine, the Neckar flows quietly and slowly through Heidelberg, where it has carved out the deepest part of its valley between hills that are more than 400 metres high. However, it was not always gentle, as the word "Neckar" itself suggests. The name is of Celtic origin and means "wild water". It was not until its conversion to a river navigation in the 1920s that the river was tamed in its course, and the frequent changes in water level and the numerous cliffs no longer presented a problem to shipping.

www.weisse-flotte-heidelberg.de

MADE BY HEIDELBERG

Print Media Academy and (S)printing Horse are just two of many emblems of Heidelberg that show its status as a dynamic place of business: Heidelberg is more than a tourist attraction. Companies that are based here include global leaders such as HeidelbergCement AG, a major supplier of building materials;

Heidelberger Druckmaschinen AG, known all over the world for its offset printing machines; Technology group ABB Stotz-Kontakt, a supplier of safety automation; big names in the IT industry such as SAP and the SAS Institute; and the ProMinent-Group, an international leader in water technology. Here Lamy produces pens that have won awards all over the world, and WILD makes a popular fruit drink called Capri-Sun. Heidelberg is also home to Springer Nature, a global academic publishing company.

streets. To experience a bit of the romantic side of Heidelberg's student scene, go to one of the historic *student pubs* such as the Roter Ochse or Zum Seppl. Germany's longest-established student jazz club, Cave 54, is also to be found in the Old Town. Sip a cocktail in the Bent Bar at Neckarmünzplatz. And on a warm summer evening, try *locations on the Neckar* such as Heidelbeach in Neuenheim, Pier 4 below the Stadthalle or the Bootshaus, the club pub of the Heidelberg rowing society.

When the pubs close, the *dance clubs* are just getting going. There are lots of places to dance the night away, from small clubs in the Old Town to music clubs on Bergheimer Straße such as Billy Blues and Halle02 in the Bahnstadt or the Kulturhaus Karlstorbahnhof.

Day 2

The Castle

ROMANTIC HEIDELBERG

The picturesque castle ruin inspired the Romantics, delighted countless students who came to the university after its reorganisation, and was celebrated by visitors as a place where a glorified view of the past had visibly found its home. For people of the Romantic age, Heidelberg was the incarnation of the ideal town. Clemens Brentano, Achim von Arnim, Joseph von Görres und Joseph von Eichendorff praised the town in song and poetry, and painters such as Karl Philipp Fohr and J.M.W. Turner depicted the ruin in famous pictures. If you would like to find out more about the reception of the castle in the Romantic age, visit the permanent exhibition in the Ruprechtsbau.

TESTIMONY TO A GLORIOUS PAST – THE CASTLE

The ascent of the Königstuhl takes you to one of Europe's best-known ruined castles, the centre of power and prestige of the prince electors for five centuries and, thanks to the enthusiasm of 19th-century Romantics, the emblem of Heidelberg.

When Elector Ruprecht III (reigned 1398–1410) extended an early 13th-century castle to make it his seat of power, he laid the foundation for a splendid palace. Continually enlarged by his successors, over the centuries it became an architectural ensemble with some of the finest Renaissance buildings in Germany. Its history did not end until the War of the Palatinate Succession, when French troops destroyed the castle after capturing the town, and Prince Elector Karl Philipp moved his residence to Mannheim in 1720. If a French aristocrat, Count Charles de Graimberg (➤ p. 10), had not campaigned for the preservation of the castle ruins and made views of them known all over the world through prints, only a few stones would remain today.

THE WITCH'S BITE

Look out for the thick iron knocker, a ring on the little door that has been cut out of the wooden gate at the entrance for security reasons. The small hollow in the iron is said to derive from the bite of a witch! As one of the prince electors had no children to succeed him, according to a legend he promised power to whoever could bite through the thick knocker on the door. If anyone was strong enough to do so, he believed, they would also be strong enough to rule. Many noblemen tried it, but it was a witch who almost succeeded, until at the last moment her teeth fell out.

The easiest way to go up to the castle is to take the funicular railway. Before starting the castle tour, it is worth making a short detour to the Stückgarten, so called because it was laid out for the cannon (Stücke) of Elector Ludwig V (reigned 1508–44). Because this spot commands a beautiful view of Heidelberg, Elector Friedrich V demolished the greater part of the fortifications here in 1615 and created a pleasure garden with a gate like a triumphal arch, the Elisabethentor, as a gift for his wife Elizabeth Stuart on her 19th birthday.

To reach the castle courtyard you have to cross the Hirschgraben (Stag Ditch), in which stags

1 Großer Altan
   (castle terrace)
2 Dicker Turm
3 Fassbau
4 Friedrichsbau
5 Gläserner Saalbau
6 Frauenzimmerbau
7 Ottheinrichsbau and
   Apothekermuseum
8 Bibliotheksbau
9 Ruprechtsbau
10 Torturm mit Hexenring
11 Krautturm
12 Fountain with
   Father Rhine
13 Visitor Centre

THE GREAT BARREL

In front of the façade of the Friedrichsbau you descend at an angle on the left to the wine cellar of the electors, home to the Großes Fass, one of the castle's main attractions. This barrel, built for Elector Karl Theodor (reigned 1742-99) by his cellarer Johann Jakob Englert using 90 oak trees from the forests of the Palatinate,

holds some 220,000 litres. After being used three times it started to leak and was never filled again. Like its three predecessors, the barrel, which is seven metres wide and 8.5 metres long, supports a dance floor on which the court could hold merry celebrations. The wine cellar itself dates from the period of the first barrel, when Elector Johann Casimir (reigned 1588–93) ordered construction of a barrel "like no other on earth" with a capacity of almost 128,000 litres.

and bears were kept in the 17th century, passing through the house of the bridge keeper and going over a stone bridge to a rectangular gate tower with a heavy wooden door. The oldest residential building in the castle, the Ruprechtsbau, built for Elector Ruprecht III (reigned 1398–1410), is on the left in the courtyard. A coat of arms with the imperial eagle is a reference to the fact that this prince elector was also king of the Germans, with the title Ruprecht I of the Palatinate. Above the entrance you see two angels with a wreath of five roses. According to tradition this commemorates two sons of a master builder who were killed during construction work. The grieving father became a recluse and brought a fresh wreath of roses to the construction site every day until his sons appeared to him in a dream and consoled him. From that moment he returned to the job and immortalised his children in stone.

Next to it is the late-Gothic Bibliotheksbau (library) with its fine oriel on the upper floor, built in the reign of Elector Ludwig V (1508–1544). The adjacent Frauenzimmerbau, of which only the

Have a break

After your visit, take refreshments offered by the **Heidelberger Schloss Restaurants & Events GmbH** on the terrace in front of the old domestic buildings or in the historic bakery.
www.heidelberger-schloss-gastronomie.de

ground floor remains, probably accommodated ladies of court on its upper floors, while the great royal hall beneath was used for daily meals and festivities. Today it is used as a hall for events.

> **3 TIP** Don't fail to put your foot in the Rittersprung (knight's leap)! This foot-shaped depression in the stone is said to be the print of a young nobleman who was caught in flagrante with the young wife of an elector and made his escape by jumping from a window. It is said that anyone whose foot fits into the hole will have a happy life.

On the north side of the courtyard stands the magnificent Friedrichsbau. The elector who built it, Friedrich IV (reigned 1583–1610), adorned its façade with his ancestors from the House of Wittelsbach – from Charlemagne to Ludwig of Bavaria – in order to legitimise his rule. The castle chapel on the ground floor escaped destruction and is used for weddings today. To the right of the Friedrichsbau a passage leads to the Altan, a terrace with a view of the valley. From here you have a superb panorama of Heidelberg's Old Town, the river Neckar and its valley down towards the plain of the Rhine.

To the right of the entrance you see the Gläserner Saalbau with its massive arches dating from the time of Elector Friedrich II (reigned 1544–56). The building takes its name (Glass Hall) from the Venetian mirrors that embellished

PERKEO

Opposite the Great Barrel is a painted wooden figure of the famous dwarf Perkeo, whom visitors to Heidelberg encounter in many places. Elector Karl Philipp is said to have brought a hard-drinking dwarf named Clemens from Tyrol to his court to be his steward and master of ceremonies. As the court dwarf responded to every offer of a drink with the words "Perche No?" ("Why not?"), he quickly acquired his nickname. His ability to hold his drink was so famous that he was celebrated in many poems. Viktor von Scheffel wrote:
"The dwarf Perkeo
At Heidelberg's court
Is a giant at drinking
Though his stature
is short."
Perkeo is reported by legend to have died in his eighties because he took the doctor's advice to drink a glass of water instead of wine, and died of dysentery.

the hall on the upper floor. A few years later Elector Ottheinrich (reigned 1556-59) constructed the Ottheinrichsbau on the east side. Its elaborate courtly façade is regarded as one of the finest examples of Renaissance architecture in Germany. Framed by two staircase towers and adorned with a portal in the form of a triumphal arch, it is impressive above all for the rich sculptural work on the façade showing figures from the Bible and ancient times to symbolise the rule of the prince elector. This and the adjoining building are now home to a museum of pharmacy, the Deutsches Apotheken-Museum.

◆ *10am-6pm (Apr-Oct)*
10am-5.30pm (Nov-Mar)
www.deutsches-apotheken-museum.de

Before leaving the castle it is worth taking a walk past the Krautturm, a tower with masonry that was blown up by the French, through the large palace garden, the Hortus Palatinus, which occupies five terraces high above the Neckar. When the garden was created (1615–19) it was regarded as one of the leading examples of Renaissance horticulture, an eighth wonder of the world. Today only a few details such as the big grotto with Father Rhine testify to past glories. Finish your visit by standing on the Scheffelterrasse in the north-east of the garden to enjoy the view of the castle ruins and the valley of the Neckar.

Schlosshof 1 (Königstuhl)
▲ *Bergbahn* ◆ *9am-8pm (Apr-Oct),*
9am-5.30pm (Nov-Mar)
www.schloss-heidelberg.de

KÖNIGSTUHL: Fit walkers take the Himmelsleiter (heavenly ladder) from Kornmarkt, a picturesque stairway built in 1844 with about 1,600 steps, but most people take the Bergbahn (funicular railway) via the stations Schloss and Molkenkur to the top of the Königstuhl.

At 567.8 metres it is the highest point in the Kleiner Odenwald, with a wonderful view of the Neckar valley, the plain of the Rhine and in good weather as far as Alsace. Here you can walk on various trails, take children to discover Snow White and other fairytale figures in the *Märchenparadies* and watch birds of prey in the *Falknerei Tinnunculus*.

www.maerchen-paradies.de
www.tinnunculus-heidelberg.de

Philosophers' Path

3 to May

University

City Walk

Heidelberg by Night

Kurpfälzisches Museum

The Castle

Schwetzingen Palace

Strolling and Shopping

Philosophers' Path

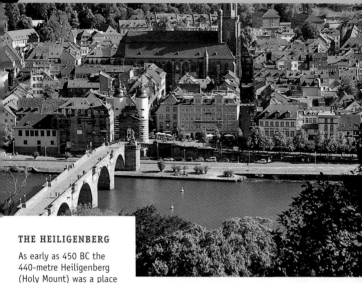

THE HEILIGENBERG

As early as 450 BC the 440-metre Heiligenberg (Holy Mount) was a place of settlement. Around the summit Celts built an encircling wall five kilometres long as a defence against the advance of Germanic peoples. This is now one of the largest extant Celtic fortifications and is still visible on the ground. The Heidenloch (Heathen Hole), a 50-metre-deep shaft that is shrouded in myth, was probably used for religious purposes. In the Nazi period the hill was deprived of its Celtic connection and hailed as a "Germanic cult site". In 1934 the Thingstätte (a "Thing" was an ancient Germanic place of assembly) was constructed here with 8,000 seats and standing room for a further 5,000 persons. It has survived, as has the early Romanesque ruin of St Michael's and St Stephen's monastery.

IN THE FOOTSTEPS OF POETS AND THINKERS – THE PHILOSOPHERS' PATH

The walk called Philosophenweg crosses the Neckar and follows one of Germany's most beautiful paths, commanding a magnificent panoramic view of the castle and the Old Town of Heidelberg.

It makes no real difference where you begin the three-kilometre walk, as you have to climb 120 metres whichever option you decide to take, but the gentle ascent, most suitable for people who are not experienced walkers, starts in the Neuenheim district of the town. From Laden-

burger Straße the path climbs in steep curves to a point halfway up the Heiligenberg, passing the Physikalisches Institut of the university and some fine detached houses with gardens full of trees, which you can stop to admire. When you have reached house no. 21 you can breathe a sigh of relief, as the climb is over and you are rewarded with a first lovely view of the Kongresshalle and restaurant ship.

In 1841, when this path through the vineyards was widened, no-one could have imagined that it would become one of Germany's most famous walks. It gained its name in the Romantic period, when young philosophers, as students were then called because they had to study philosophy for several terms before the beginning of their specialised courses, used to meet here for a romantic stroll or an undisturbed tête-à-tête. Poets and thinkers such as Hölderlin, Eichendorff, Scheffel and many others came here to relax, and walked through the vineyards to give free rein to their thoughts.

The first stop, where the Bismarcksäulenweg branches off, is a reminder of this era: the *Philosophengärtchen*, a little garden with flower beds where stands a bust of the Romantic poet

Eichendorff with one of his verses inscribed on the plinth. Here you can stop for a while to enjoy the panorama of the castle, Königstuhl, Old Town and river Neckar. A small kiosk at the crossing of the paths sells refreshing drinks.

Above the path, and as far as Liselotteplatz, exotic plants, bushes and trees such as cork oak, jasmine, broom and the indigo bush have been planted. In spring and summer they spread a wonderful fragrance. Further on too you will be surprised again and again by Mediterranean plants and trees in the gardens along the way. It seems unusual for pomegranate, almond and lemon trees, bamboo, pines and palms to be thriving here, but this slope is one of the warmest places in Germany. Its south-facing aspect, its steep gradient of up to 45 degrees and the warming effect of downslope winds create special

BISMARCK COLUMN

There is another fine view from the lookout platform of the Bismarcksäule. The upper path that branches off at the Philosophengärtchen leads there. The Bismarck Column in Heidelberg dates from 1903, when such towers were erected all over Germany to honour the founder of the Reich, Otto von Bismarck. The architect Wilhelm Kreis produced a standard design for them named "twilight of the gods", and this version was used in Heidelberg. The 15-metre-high square tower of red sandstone with three-quarter columns at the corners is adorned on the side facing the town by a relief of the imperial eagle with the snake of discord. At the top of the tower is a cast-iron cauldron with a diameter of 2.5 metres, used by student fraternities to light a fire on certain days of the year such as Bismarck's birthday.

I LOST MY HEART IN HEIDELBERG

The catchy tune that Fred Raymond composed in 1927 for lyrics by Fritz Löhner-Beda and Ernst Neubach is just one example of many songs and poems about Heidelberg. In 1800 Friedrich Hölderlin hailed Heidelberg in an ode as "the most beautiful city in all the fatherland", in 1855 Joseph von Eichendorff sang of his arrival in Heidelberg, and in 1854 Joseph Victor von Scheffel celebrated the town in his student song "Old Heidelberg, thou city fine, ...None compares with thee", while Kurt Tucholsky parodied them all and Heidelberg's reputation: "the loveliest place that here on earth is mine, Heidelberg in Vienna on the Rhine". Few cities have been praised in song as much as Heidelberg.

climatic conditions, and the average temperature is about 1.5 degrees Celsius higher than down in the town. This is the reason why wild bees, which like the warmth, find a congenial habitat here, as an information board explains. With a little luck, on a warm day you will spot wall lizards sunning themselves on one of the many dry-stone walls that border the path.

The shelter on *Liselotteplatz*, where a memorial stone commemorates Liselotte von der Pfalz, the sister-in-law of King Louis XIV of France, is especially popular as a place to stop for younger walkers, as there is a playground. You can work out what has changed in the panorama of Heidelberg since Matthäus Merian made his famous copperplate engraving in 1820 by studying the information board at the *Merianausblick*.

Before descending, continue to the *Hölderlin-Anlage*, a beautiful garden with a memorial to the poet Hölderlin on the spot where the hamlet of Dagersbach and its church once stood.

The path down passes between mossy old walls on the narrow *Schlangenweg*, which snakes down the slope, sometimes in the form of steps. In many places lookout points invite you to stop and admire the lovely view once again. At the end of the descent, cross Neuenheimer Landstraße and the Alte Brücke to return to the Old Town.

Strolling and Shopping

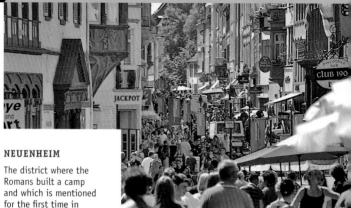

NEUENHEIM

The district where the Romans built a camp and which is mentioned for the first time in the year 765 in the Lorsch Codex is older than Heidelberg itself. Once a farming and fishing village, it was incorporated into the

town in 1891. Its idyllic character, its situation on the banks of the Neckar, proximity to the Old Town and many attractive dwellings make Neuenheim, with more than 13,000 residents, a sought-after place to live. It is best known for its university campus at Neuenheimer Feld. The Physikalisches Institut moved to Philosophenweg back in 1912, and since the 1950s scientific institutions, the university clinic, major research institutes and the Technologiepark have come to the west of Neuenheim.

STROLLING AND SHOPPING: ON AND AROUND THE HAUPTSTRASSE

Whether you plan to hunt through the outlets of well-known brand names or browse in little shops, in Heidelberg you will find appealing items for all tastes and in every price bracket.

The area that attracts most shoppers is the Old Town with its streets and alleys between Bis-

3 Days in TIP To get your bearings in Heidelberg's shopping scene, download the App *Mein Heidelberg* free of charge from the AppStore or Android Market.

marckplatz and Kornmarkt. Heidelberg's number-one shopping street is the *Hauptstraße* (Main Street), which is described as one of Europe's

loveliest pedestrian zones thanks to its location at the heart of the Old Town. At Bismarckplatz the Darmstädter Hof, the town's biggest shopping centre, and the four-storey Galeria Kaufhof department store mark the start of a shopping zone where all the famous names and brands of the national and international retail scene rub shoulders on a shopping street over one kilometre long.

If you prefer something more individual, walk through the side alleys and *Plöck*, which is parallel to the Hauptstraße, or *Untere Straße*. Here lots of little shops run by the owners sell unusual clothing, nice gifts and products from all around the world. In between them cafés and restaurants invite you to stop for a break, and when the sun shines you feel as if you were in the Mediterranean. Antique dealers and galleries have found

Have a break

To drink some hot chocolate or coffee and try home-made chocolate specialities or ice cream, go to **Chocolaterie St. Anna No 1**.

St. Anna Gasse 1 ♦ Mon-Sat 10am-8pm, Sun 11am-8pm

STADTHALLE

There is space for about 3,500 people in "Heidelberg's parlour," which was built in 1903 as a place for the citizens to assemble and hold festivities. The charms of this sandstone building on the banks of the Neckar are its delicate Art Nouveau doors at the main entrance, elaborate sculptural decoration such as the portraits of important Heidelberg personalities on the window arches, the head of Heidelberga above the main

entrance, busts of Reich Chancellor Otto von Bismarck and the military strategist Helmuth von Moltke on the east façade, and the coats of arms of the eight largest cities in Baden on the north and south façades. Inside, the Stadthalle reveals itself to be a modern congress and arts centre that can be used for many purposes.

Neckarstaden 24
▲ Kongresshaus,
www.heidelberg-
kongresshaus.de

KNOWLEDGE CREATES THE CITY ...

... is the title of the Internationale Bauausstellung (International Building Exhibition), which is taking place in Heidelberg from 2012 to 2022. This is not an exhibition in the usual sense, but a German event for construction and urban planning with a tradition going back more than 100 years. Its aim is to provide major impulses for urban development through new ideas and projects over a ten-year period. This was the origin of, for example, the Mathildenhöhe artists' colony in Darmstadt in 1901 and the Weissenhofsiedlung in Stuttgart in 1927. In Heidelberg the aim is to find scope for design and model solutions for the city of the future, as the city and science are inextricably connected here. In this way Heidelberg can make its mark even more clearly as an international location for science and become a "European model city for the knowledge-based society of the 21st century".

www.heidelberg.de/iba

a home in a street parallel to the Hauptstraße, Friedrich-Ebert-Anlage, which is worth strolling along if only for its fine historic townhouses.

If you walk across the Neckar bridge from Bismarckplatz, in good weather you will not only see the sunbathers on the grass by the riverbank but also reach the attractive district of *Neuenheim*. Here, around Brückenstraße, many small shops with individual service cover all aspects of daily life, selling fashion, jewellery, flowers, toys, books and much more. On Wednesdays and Saturdays a food market is held on Neuenheimer Marktplatz, where the late Gothic tower of old St John's Church can be seen.

Have a break

When the sun shines, **Bar Centrale** on the marketplace puts its chairs and tables outside so that guests can drink an espresso or eat a snack away from the crowds of tourists.
Ladenburger Straße 17 ◆ Mon-Thu 8-1am, Fri-Sat 8-3am, Sun 9-1am

Schwetzingen Palace

City Walk

University

Heidelberg by Night

Kurpfälzisches Museum

3 Days in

The Castle

Schwetzingen Palace

Philosophers' Path

Strolling and Shopping

ORIGINS OF THE PALACE

In 1350 a small moated castle was built on this site. Over the centuries it was rebuilt and destroyed several times. It owes its present Baroque appearance to Prince Elector Johann Wilhelm (1658–1716), who made it into a palace with three wings around a court of honour. When the summer residence of the court was moved from Mannheim to Schwetzingen under Elector Carl Philipp (1661–1741), the golden age of the palace began. His successor Carl Theodor (1724–99) extended Schloss Schwetzingen, built the court theatre and had the gardens newly laid out. Today the palace is owned by the federal state of Baden-Württemberg.

THE PRINCE ELECTORS' SUMMER RESIDENCE – SCHWETZINGEN PALACE

A visit to this Baroque palace ensemble takes you to a magnificent garden, a cultural heritage site of European significance.

Before you stroll through the palace garden, take time to visit the former state rooms and living apartments of the prince electors, which are furnished with authentic 18th-century items. On the courtyard side are the single-storey curved buildings called the Zirkelbauten, which were used for the court's games, concerts and balls.

Adjoining the North Zirkelbau and Orangery is the court theatre, built by Nicolas de Pigage. It was the first theatre in Germany to have tiered seating.

The palace gardens, among the most beautiful in Germany, are a masterpiece of late Baroque garden design. The front section was designed by the architect Nicolas de Pigage in the style of a French Baroque garden, while Friedrich Ludwig von Sckell, who created the rear section, took his inspiration from English landscape parks. The existence side by side of two completely different styles makes a walk through the gardens particularly enjoyable.

The palace terrace commands a wonderful view of the strictly geometrical French-style Baroque garden, which is aligned with the central axis of the palace. A broad path that leads to the circular central parterre and the Arion Fountain emphasises this symmetry. To the right and left in parterres and bosquets are sculptures, small ponds, fountains and temples. The Natural Theatre, used for small-scale outdoor performances, is picturesquely integrated into the garden in a grotto. In the background the circular Temple of Apollo rises on a small mound, with a depiction of the god of the arts holding his lyre. Continue a little way to the

PRINCE ELECTORS

The title of "prince elector" ("Kurfürst") was held by those princes of the Holy Roman Empire who from the 13th century had the right to elect the king of the Germans. This right gave the prince electors a leading position in the empire. The electoral college consisted initially of seven, later of nine electors. They included the counts palatinate of the Rhine, whose seat was in Heidelberg for centuries and who had electoral rights because they were considered to be of particularly high status, as their territory lay in the area of the old Frankish kingdom.

1 Court of honour with guard building, main entrance
2 Main palace building
3 Palace terrace
4 South Zirkelbau
5 North Zirkelbau
6 Rococo theatre
7 Invalids' barracks
8 Arion Fountain
9 Temple of Minerva and triton fountain
10 Avenue of urns with Lycian Apollo
11 Orangery and orangery garden
12 Natural Theatre
13 Temple of Apollo
14 Bathhouse and Wild Boar Grotto
15 Teahouse and Water Bell
16 Water-spouting birds
17 Arboretum and Baroque gates
18 Roman water fort with aqueduct
19 English Garden
20 Chinese Bridge
21 Great Pond
22 Rhine and Danube river gods
23 Temple of Mercury
24 Mosque pond
25 Mosque and Turkish Garden

150 m

SCHWETZINGEN SWR FESTIVAL

For more than 60 years Schloss Schwetzingen has provided a stage for classical music from April to June. Under the motto "rediscover the old, initiate the new, give young talent an opportunity," the varied programme includes a total of 50 concerts (some of them held in churches in the nearby city of Speyer) and two opera productions. In the historic court theatre an opera is usually staged by a well-known opera house, and a newly commissioned work or an unknown opera from the Baroque or Classical period is given a premiere. Established artists and talented young musicians present concerts of chamber and orchestral music, piano and lieder evenings, all of them broadcast by SWR2 radio. With some 550 radio broadcasts per year worldwide, the festival is also the biggest radio festival of classical music.

www.schwetzinger-swr-festspiele.de

Bathhouse, a private refuge for the prince elector where an oval room at the centre is decorated by a ceiling painting of the goddess Aurora, and take a look at the fountain with birds spouting water in the garden in front of it.

From the palace you can see the large lake at the end of the gardens. It is adorned by the gods of the rivers Rhine and Danube on the steps. If you walk over the Chinese Bridge you pass the lake and reach the English Garden, which lies to the west and northwest. The majestic artificial ruin that rises in the landscape is the Temple of Mercury. From its upper floor there is a wonderful view across the lake to the Red Mosque, which was not intended to be an Islamic place of worship but to express the principle of tolerance towards all the religions and cultures of the world. This domed building with its minarets can be seen above the water of the mosque lake, with the Turkish Garden and a large ambulatory with prayer niches carved in wood and pavilions.

▲ *Schloss (Rhein-NeckarBus 717 towards Speyer)*
◆ *9am-7.30pm (Apr-Oct), 9am-4.30pm (Nov-Mar), visits inside the palace only as part of a guided tour, every hour Mon-Fri 11am-4pm, Sat-Sun 10.30am-5pm, see www.schloss-schwetzingen.de/en/visitor-information/*

Have a break

Enjoy the princely surroundings of the **Schloss-restaurant Schwetzingen** inside the North Zirkelbau or on the terrace in front of it.
◆ *10am-7.30pm*

Kurpfälzisches Museum

ZOO

A trip to Heidelberg Zoo, which was founded in 1934 by the Nobel laureate Carl Bosch and the ornithologist Otto Fehringer, is a popular outing for the whole family. According to the motto "see life live" visitors can get up close to impressive lions, tigers and bears amongst fine old trees, watch South American sea lions doing their tricks, admire the flight of giant sea eagles

and discover shyer animals such as snakes, toads and hedgehogs at the midday demonstration. Among the highlights are the extensive elephant compound and the new elephant house, in which the first group of young male elephants in a German zoo, consisting of four lively young bulls, is at home.

Tiergartenstraße 3
▲ *Zoo*
◆ *9am-7pm (Apr-Sep),*
9am-6pm (Mar, Oct),
9am-5pm (Nov-Feb)
www.zoo-heidelberg.de

CENTURIES OF HISTORY – KURPFÄLZISCHES MUSEUM

A visit to the old Palais Morass immerses you deeply in the history of what used to be the Electoral Palatinate. You can make the acquaintance of the prince electors and their wives and admire the magnificence of their court life.

It is owing to the French émigré Charles de Graimberg and his extensive collection of paintings, prints, documents, coins, weapons, porcelain, sculptures and architectural fragments that Heidelberg possesses such an interesting museum today. After his death the town bought the collection in 1879, and from 1908 put it on display in the Baroque palais of Philipp Morass, a law professor. Thanks to archaeological finds, generous donations and purchases, visitors can take a historical trip from the earliest times to the 20th century.

Exciting discoveries await on a circuit of the museum, even though visitors may sometimes think they have lost their bearings as they follow a complicated path through the building and its wings.

BOTANICAL GARDEN

Founded in 1593 as the hortus medicus of the university, a garden for healing plants, the Botanischer Garten in Neuenheimer Feld is not only a place of relaxation where visitors come to stroll. It is used for scientific research and teaching, as a place where species threatened with extinc-

Surprising artistic highlights keep appearing, from Tilman Riemenschneider's *Altar of the Apostles* dating from 1509, a tondo by Lucas Cranach the Elder depicting *Adam and Eve at the Fall of Man* (1525) and a *Madonna and Child* by Rogier van der Weyden (painted on wood, c 1455) to an opulently laid dinner table with a 72-piece silver service from Strasbourg that belonged to Elisabeth Augusta (1721–94), the last electoral princess. Reception and living rooms entirely fitted with period furniture, porcelain and paintings convey an impression of the life of the periods

represented, and a gallery of dynastic paintings in the entrance area, with life-size portraits of Friedrich V and his consort Elizabeth Stuart, a portrait of Liselotte von der Pfalz in old age and a likeness of the court jester Perkeo, bring the history of the now-vanished Electoral Palatinate back to life.

To find out about the age of the bourgeoisie and the story of Heidelberg after 1800, take a look at the exhibition on Heidelberg in the Romantic age and the later 19th century on the ground floor.

Individual works and series from the prints collection show how the castle and town were depicted in the Romantic era. Fans of Dutch painting will be delighted by the Posselt Collection, which presents some 150 portraits, landscapes, genre scenes and still-lifes on wine-red walls.

tion can be protected and as a place for public education. About 10,000 kinds of plants are cultivated in the hothouses and out in the open. The most significant collections are the orchids and bromeliads, as well as the currently largest European collection of dry plants from Madagascar.

Im Neuenheimer Feld 340 (Neuenheim)
▲ *Botanischer Garten botgart.hip. uni-heidelberg.de*

STIFT NEUBURG

Go back in time on a visit to the historic Stift Neuburg, a Benedictine Abbey which was a favourite rendezvous of the Romantics after its dissolution in 1804. Where Carl Maria von Weber was inspired to compose his opera *Der Freischütz*, and where Schlegel, Brentano, Görres and Rilke admired the abbey's beautiful site on a slope amid green meadows between Neuenheim and Ziegelhausen, since 1927 there has once again been a community of Benedictine monks. Today visitors can find a retreat in the monastery guesthouse for a few days, buy farm produce in the shop or try the monks' beer in the lovely beer garden.

Stiftweg 2-4 (Ziegelhausen),
▲ *Stift Neuburg*
www.klosterhof-neuburg.de

To go back to the early days of humanity, descend to the cellar, where a tour of the archaeological department begins with a copy of the lower jaw of Homo heidelbergensis (➤ p. 64). Here dioramas recreate the everyday life of a Neolithic family. Finds from excavations, the reconstruction of the Heidelberg Mithraeum and a Roman dining room tell the story of life in a Roman province. In the room with finds from excavations on Kornmarkt, a reconstructed kitchen with a hearth and furniture depicts life in Heidelberg around the year 1600. The lapidarium, a collection of stones related to the town's history with medieval epitaphs, the original sculptures from the Alte Brücke, the figure of Hercules from the well on the marketplace and other items, has found its place in the massive cellar vaults.

Hauptstraße 97
▲ *Kongresshaus/Stadthalle, Universitätsplatz, Peterskirche*
◆ *Tue-Sun 10am-6pm*
www.museum-heidelberg.de

Have a break

After all this art and history, the **restaurant** in the charming museum courtyard offers a welcome break with Italian food.
Restaurant Kurpfälzisches Museum, Hauptstraße 97 ◆ *11am-11pm*

Accommodation, Going Out, Tips and Addresses

Hotels

SKYLABS

SKYLABS, an ultra-low-energy building that provides approximately 19,500 square metres of space for research and laboratories, lies in the middle of the new technology campus of the Bahnstadt district. Its two five-storey buildings and a nine-storey tower with projecting upper floors make it stand out from its surroundings as a conspicuous symbol of pioneering connections between science

and business. As a new quarter of science-based high-tech companies, the campus has central facilities in order to enable companies from the biotechnology and pharmacology sectors to complete pre-clinical tests.

www.sky-labs.de

LOW BUDGET

● **HOTEL GARNI AM KORNMARKT****
Kornmarkt 7 (Old Town)
tel. 06221/905830
▲ Bergbahn/Rathaus
www.hotelamkornmarkt.de

Pleasant little hotel with a wonderful red Baroque façade right on Kornmarkt.

● **LOTTE – THE BACKPACKERS**
Hostel Heidelberg
Burgweg 3 (Old Town)
tel. 06221/7350725
▲ Bergbahn/Rathaus
www.lotte-heidelberg.de

Hostel with modern rooms in one of the town's oldest buildings, directly beneath the castle.

● **STEFFI'S HOSTEL HEIDELBERG**
Alte Eppelheimer Straße 50
tel. 06221/7782772
▲ Hauptbahnhof
www.hostelheidelberg.de

Hostel welcomes backpackers from all over the world in a friendly and green oasis located just metres from the main station.

ECONOMY

● **ARTHOTEL HEIDELBERG******
Grabengasse 7 (Old Town)
tel. 06221/650060
▲ Universitätsplatz
www.arthotel.de

Near the university and in the heart of the Old Town, an architecturally appealing hotel thanks to its combination of a protected historic building with a modern addition.

● **BERGHEIM 41**
Hotel im Alten Hallenbad
Bergheimer Straße 41 (Bergheim)
tel. 06221/750040
▲ Bismarckplatz
www.bergheim41.de

This modern city hotel in the Altes Hallenbad, an old swimming pool complex mixing Art Nouveau and Classical styles, is close to Bismarckplatz and boasts a roof garden with a view of the castle.

● **HOLLÄNDER HOF*****ˢ
Neckarstaden 66 (Old Town)
tel. 06221/60500
▲ Marstallstraße
www.hollaender-hof.de

Romantic hotel with a superb view of the Alte Brücke, the Neckar and Philosophenweg.

● **HOTEL "CAFÉ FRISCH"**
Jahnstraße 34
(Neuenheim)
tel. 06221/45750
▲ Jahnstraße
www.cafe-frisch.de

Family-run accommodation right by the Neckar near the university clinic and the research facilities in Neuenheimer Feld, popular for the in-house bakery.

● **MARRIOTT HEIDELBERG★★★★**
Vangerowstraße 16
tel. 06221/9080
▲ Betriebshof
www.marriott.de

Business hotel on the banks of the Neckar, at the approach to the town, close to Bahnstadt and convenient for the autobahn.

● **QUBE HOTEL HEIDELBERG**
Bergheimer Straße 74
(Bergheim)
tel. 06221/187990
▲ Römerstraße
www.qube-hotel-heidelberg.de

Privately run design hotel near the station with an award-winning restaurant.

SUPERIOR

● **HEIDELBERG SUITES★★★★★**
Neuenheimer
Landstraße 12 (Old Town)
tel. 06221/655650
▲ Alte Brücke Nord
www.heidelbergsuites.com

Near the university and in the heart of the Old Town, an architecturally appealing hotel thanks to its combination of a protected historic building with a modern addition.

● **VILLA MARSTALL★★★★+**
Lauerstraße 1 (Old Town)
tel. 06221/655570
▲ Marstallstraße
www.villamarstall.de

Attractive hotel in a late Classical townhouse in the Old Town, right by the Neckar with a view of the castle, Alte Brücke and Philosophenweg.

BAHNSTADT

Cities can change their appearance quickly – as demonstrated by the new quarter that is now arising on the site of a former rail freight yard between the districts Weststadt and Pfaffengrund. Here a "City of Knowledge" is being conceived, with everything that scientists need to live and work. On an area of 116 hectares, larger than Heidelberg's Old Town, this new quarter makes space available for scientific work, accommodation, enjoying life, art and culture. There is housing for 6,500 people and places of work up to 6,000. The energy planning also looks to the future, as it will be Europe's largest district of sustainable "passive buildings" with ultra-low energy consumption.

www.heidelberg-bahnstadt.de

Restaurants

HEIDELBERG SPECIALITIES

Apfelküchle:
pancakes with slices of apples, to which are added sugar and cinnamon or custard.

Buwespitzle:
(also called Schupf-nudeln): a mix of potato, egg, flour and butter, pressed into pasta shape and fried.

Handkäs mit Musik:
ripe sour-milk cheese marinated in chopped onions with vinegar, oil, caraway seeds, pepper and salt.

Kartäuserklösse:
a poor man's dish made of stale bread rolls soaked in milk with sugar and egg white, dipped in flour then fried and sprinkled with sugar and cinnamon.

● **DAS BOOTSHAUS**
Schurmanstraße 2
tel. 06221/25396
▲ Thibautstraße
◆ Sun-Fri from 11.30am,
Sat from 5pm
www.dasbootshaus.com

The former boathouse of the Heidelberg rowing club has a sunny terrace with a direct view of the Neckar, where meals inspired by the Pacific region and Asia are served.

DIE KUH DIE LACHT
Hauptstraße 133
(Old Town)
tel. 06221/7276455
▲ Alte Brücke
◆ Mon-Thu 11.30 am-10pm, Fri-Sat 11.30am-11pm, Sun noon-9pm
www.diekuhdielacht.com

A tip for all burger lovers: there is a wide choice here, all of it with seasonal, fresh ingredients!

● **HUGO WINE & DINE**
Rohrbacher Straße 47
tel. 06221/5860120
▲ Hans-Böckler-Straße, Kaiserstraße
◆ Mon 10am-5pm,
Tue-Fri 10am-midnight,
Sat 5pm-midnight
www.hugo-hd.de

The in-house wine shop is not the only reason to come to this restaurant with a Mediterranean atmosphere and a creative menu.

● **LE COQ**
Brückenstraße 17
(Neuenheim)
tel. 06221/6736791
▲ Brückenstraße
◆ Tue-Fri 10am-2.30pm, 6-10pm, Sat 10am-10pm, Sun 10am-9pm
www.lecoq-hd.de

A pleasant place with a casual atmosphere to spend an evening enjoying classic French food and more.

● **OSKAR**
Haspelgasse 5 (Old Town)
tel. 06221/4319034
▲ Marstallstraße
◆ Mon-Sat from 6pm
www.oskar-hd.de

Here you can enjoy German and Mediterranean dishes with a glass of good wine.

● PICCOLO MONDO
Klingenteichstraße 6
▲ Peterskirche
◆ Wed-Sun noon-3pm,
6-11pm
www.piccolomondo-heidelberg.de

A wonderful place for
lovers of Italian food.

● RESTAURANT QUBE
Bergheimer Straße 74
(Bergheim)
tel. 06221/7187990
▲ Römerstraße
◆ Mon-Wed noon-1am,
Thu-Sat noon-2pm,
Sun noon-midnight
www.qube-hotel-heidelberg.de

Spoil yourself with imagina-
tive herbal cuisine and top-
class regional products!

● RED - DIE GRÜNE KÜCHE
Poststraße 42
tel. 06221/9145206
◆ Mon-Sat 11.30am-10pm
www.red-diegruenekueche.com

Parsnip foam soup, blood-
orange and chilli chutney
– this restaurant serves
vegetarian treats.

● RESTAURANT ROMER
Grabengasse 7
tel. 06221/65006150
▲ Universitätsplatz
◆ Mon-Sat noon-2pm,
6-10.30pm
www.arthotel.de

A combination of regional
and international dishes in
a nice surroundings.

● RESTAURANT TATI
Bergheimer Straße 151
(Bergheim)
▲ Betriebshof
◆ Mon-Sat noon-2.30pm,
6pm-midnight
www.restaurant-tati.de

If you like French cuisine,
here you will find a little
patch of France.

● SAME SAME
Steingasse 3 (Old Town)
▲ Alte Brücke
◆ Sun-Thu noon-10pm,
Fri-Sat noon-11pm
www.sushiheidelberg.de

Tiny sushi bar for fans of
raw fish.

HEIDELBERG SPECIALITIES

Kerscheplotzer or Kirschenmichel:
a bake of soaked bread
rolls with eggs, sugar,
butter, almonds, sweet
cherries and cherry
schnapps, eaten hot or
cold with or without
custard.

Maultaschen:
pasta filled with meat,
spinach, onions and
breadcrumbs.

Saumagen:
a mix of meat, bacon,
onions, chestnuts, herbs
and potatoes, cooked in
a pig's stomach.

Verheierte:
a stew of meat broth
with pieces of potato,
spätzle noodles, onions
and meat.

SERVICE

Cafés & Pubs

HEIDELBERG CALENDAR

DEC-FEB:
Winter in Schwetzingen
www.theaterheidelberg.de

FEB:
Adelante – Iberoameri-
can Theater Festival
www.adelante-festival.de
festival of cabaret and
other performing arts
www.karlstorbahnhof.de

APRIL:
Musikfestival Heidel-
berger Frühling
*www.heidelberger-
fruehling.de*

APRIL/MAY:
Heidelberger Stücke-
markt theatre festival
www.theaterheidelberg.de

JUNE:
Literature festival
www.heidellittage.de

Handschuhsheimer
Kerwe, a traditional fair
*www.tiefburg.de/
kerwe.htm*

● **CAFÉ GUNDEL**
Hauptstraße 212
(Old Town)
▲ Rathaus/Bergbahn
◆ Tue-Fri 8.30am-6.30pm,
Sat-Sun 8am-6pm
www.gundel-heidelberg.de

On the terrace with a view
of the castle you can try
out many different kinds
of cake.

● **CAFÉ KNÖSEL**
Untere Straße 37
(Old Town)
▲ Marstallstraße
◆ 8.30am-10pm
*www.cafeknösel-
heidelberg.de*

This is the town's oldest
chocolaterie, a traditional
café since 1863, where the
Heidelberg "student kiss"
was invented.

● **CAFÉ ROSSI**
Rohrbacher Straße 4
(Old Town)
▲ Bismarckplatz
◆ Mon-Thu 9am-10pm,
Fri 9am-11pm,
Sat 9am-3pm
www.caferossi.de

A vibrant place that is
always full – on Bismarckplatz, where the large old
beer garden gives you a
holiday feeling.

● **CAFÉ SCHAFHEUTLE**
Hauptstraße 94
(Old Town)
▲ Peterskirche
◆ Mon-Fri 9.30am-7pm,
Sat 9am-6pm
www.cafe-schafheutle.de

Enjoy exquisite cakes and
biscuits or delicious ice
cream with a view of the
pedestrian zone or in the
pleasant garden.

● **COFFEE NERD**
Rohrbacher Straße 9
(Old Town)
▲ Adenauerplatz
◆ Mon-Fri 9am-6pm, Sat
10am-6pm, Sun 11am-6pm
www.coffeenerd.de

A youthful coffee bar with
the obligatory racing bike
on the wall, providing
everything connected with
coffee.

● **KULTURBRAUEREI**
Leyergasse 6 (Old Town)
▲ Neckarmünzplatz
◆ Mon-Sun 11am-11pm
*www.heidelberger-kultur-
brauerei.de*

In historic brewery buildings or in the leafy courtyard, enjoy roast pork,
sauerbraten, schäufele or
crispy fried duck, washed
down with the beer
brewed on site.

● **LA TAPA**
Steingasse 16 (Old Town)
▲ Marstallstraße
◆ Tue-Fri from 6pm,
Sat-Sun from 3pm
www.la-tapa.de

A cosy place to try some
Spanish tapas over a glass
of wine.

● **MORO CAFFÉ**
Hauptstraße 160
(Old Town)
▲ Universitätsplatz
◆ Sun-Thu 9am-8pm,
Fri-Sat 9am-9pm
www.moro-cafe.de

It's a bit like being in the
Mediterranean: you can
drink espresso (or tea if
your prefer) at leisure
and eat some cake while
watching what's happen-
ing on the street.

● **SCHMELZPUNKT**
Hauptstraße 90
(Old Town)
▲ Peterskirche
◆ Mon-Fri 11am-9pm, Sat
10am-10pm,
Sun 11am-9pm
*www.schmelzpunkt-
heidelberg.de*

If you like to let home-
made ice-cream melt
in your mouth or spoil
yourself with delicate

chocolate creations, this
is the right place.

● **VETTER'S ALT HEIDEL-
BERGER BRAUHAUS**
Steingasse 9 (Old Town)
▲ Marstallstraße
◆ Sun-Thu 11.30am-mid-
night, Fri-Sat 11.30am-2am
www.brauhaus-vetter.de

Brewery in a guest house
with its own kinds of beer
and down-to-earth German
cooking.

● **ZUM GÜLDENEN SCHAF**
Hauptstraße 115
(Old Town)
▲ Universitätsplatz
◆ 11-1am
www.schaf-heidelberg.de

Old-established restaurant
with an idyllic beer garden
in the middle of the Old
Town.

**HEIDELBERG
CALENDAR**

JUNE/JULY/SEPT:
The castle illuminated
www.heidelberg-marketing.de

SUMMER:
Schlossfestspiele,
theatre and opera
festival
www.theaterheidelberg.de

SEPT:
Heidelberger Herbst,
festival in the Old Town
www.heidelberg-marketing.de

OCT:
KinderTheaterFestival
Heidelberg

OCT-NOV:
Enjoy Jazz
www.enjoyjazz.de

NOV:
Internationales
Filmfestival Mannheim-
Heidelberg
www.iffmh.de

DEC:
Christmas Market,
Christmas on Ice
on Karlsplatz
www.heidelberg-marketing.de

Bars & Nightlife

HEIDELBERG'S VITAL STATISTICS

Heidelberg has a population of nearly 160,000 and is situated near to the point where the Neckar flows into the Rhine. The city boundaries enclose an area of about 109 square kilometres, of which almost 30 per cent, or 32.2 square kilometres,

are built up and 44.2 square kilometres are woodland. The extent of the city area is approx. 13 kilometres east-west and approx. 10 kilometres north-south.

Heidelberg lies in the Upper Rhine Valley on the left bank of the Neckar in one the warmest regions in Germany, and is divided into 15 districts. Its highest point at 586 metres is the Königstuhl, and the lowest point on the river bank at Neckarsteinach lies 116 metres above sea level.

● **BAR D`AIX EN PROVENCE**
Bergstraße 1 (Neuenheim)
▲ Brückenstraße
◆ 10-3am
www.bardaix-heidelberg.de

Small bar with a French atmosphere off the tourist trail.

● **BENT BAR**
Leyergasse 2 (Old Town)
▲ Neckarmünzplatz
◆ Mon-Sat 7pm-2am
www.bentbar.de

An elegant bar in 60s and 70s style away from the bustle of the Old Town, a good place for sipping a cocktail.

● **BILLY BLUES**
Bergheimerstraße 1b (Bergheim)
▲ Bismarckplatz
◆ Wed-Thu 5pm-2am, Fri 5pm-4am, Sat 6pm-5am
www.billyblues.de

You can linger over a drink at the long bar or dance in the club to salsa and other music styles.

● **CAVE 54**
Krämergasse 2 (Old Town)
▲ Rathaus/Bergbahn
◆ Tue 8.30pm-2am, Thu 10pm-3am, Fri-Sat 10pm-5am
www.cave54.de

In Germany's oldest student club you meet people of all ages who come to dance or for concerts of jazz, blues or rock music.

● **COCKTAIL CAFÉ REGIE**
Theaterstraße 2 (Old Town)
▲ Kongresshaus
◆ Sun-Thu noon-1pm, Fri-Sat noon-3am
www.regie-heidelberg.de

These cocktail specialists will serve you 180 different cocktails, cool soft drinks and more to enjoy on the biggest outdoor terrace in the Old Town of Heidelberg.

● **HEMINGWAY'S**
Fahrtgasse 1
▲ Bismarckplatz
◆ Mon-Thu 10-1am, Fri 10-2am, Sat 9-2am, Sun 9-1am
www.hemingways-heidelberg.de

Here you can follow in the footsteps of Ernest Hemingway, relaxing with Caribbean cocktails.

● **JINX**
Untere Straße 20 (Old Town)
◆ Thu 9pm-3am, Fri-Sat 8pm-5am
www.jinx-heidelberg.de

Print Media Lounge

A cocktail bar with a club atmosphere where you can relax, celebrate and enjoy a drink.

● **KAISER**
Untere Straße 30
(Old Town)
▲ Alte Brücke
◆ Mon-Thu 7pm-2am,
Fr 7pm-4am, Sat 3pm-4am, Sun 3-9pm
www.kaiser-heidelberg.de

In the evening this cool bar changes into a dance bar the whole night.

● **ORANGE BAR**
Ingrimstraße 26
(Old Town)
▲ Alte Brücke Nord
◆ Sun-Wed 6pm-1am,
Thu 6pm-2am,
Sat-Sun 6pm-3am
www.orange-heidelberg.de

An oasis in the Old Town with the atmosphere of a living room, and the ideal

spot for a glass of wine or more.

● **PIER 4**
Neckarstaden 25
(Old Town)
▲ St. Vincentius-Krankenhaus
◆ Tue-Fri 3-11pm,
Sat-Sun noon-11pm
pier4-heidelberg.de

This swimming location on the Neckar quays below the Stadthalle is recommended for a drink with a wonderful view of the river.

● **TANGENTE**
Kettengasse 23 (Old Town)
▲ Universitätsplatz
◆ Thu 11pm-3am,
Fri-Sat 11pm-5am
www.facebook.com/pg/Tangente-Heidelberg

A small club where you can dance to the sounds of soul, funk, r'n'b, house & disco.

Alongside Mannheim and Ludwigshafen, Heidelberg is one of the three main centres of the Rhine-Neckar conurbation, which has approx. 2.36 million inhabitants. The city itself has Germany's oldest university and a population of some 49,000 students at four institutions of higher education.

Heidelberg is also the seat of the Akademie der Wissenschaften (Academy of Sciences) and several major research institutes such as the European Molecular Biology Laboratory (EMBL), the German Cancer Research Centre (DKFZ) and five Max Planck Institutes. The technology park, home to over 80 companies and research institutes, is among the leading centres of biotechnology in Germany and worldwide. Heidelberg is also a dynamic business centre where well-known firms such as Heidelberger Druckmaschinen AG, HeidelbergCement, ABB Stotz, SAP, SAS Institute and the important academic publisher Springer Nature are based.

Spas &
Fitness

PRINT MEDIA ACADEMY

When you leave the station, a 13-metre-high sculpture of a horse made of stainless steel and aluminium catches the eye. The S-Printing Horse by the sculptor Jürgen Goertz is the world's largest sculpture of a horse and symbolises the different processes in a printing works on the square in front of the communication and

know-how centre of Heidelberger Druckmaschinen AG, a manufacturer of printing machines. The 12-storey glass cube houses offices and is used for training courses that range from machine training to management seminars. The Print Media Academy also serves as a venue for congresses and conferences and has an event location on the 12th floor.

● **HALLENBAD KÖPFEL**
Stiftweg 32
tel. 06221/5132880
▲ Köpfel
◆ Mon-Wed+Fri 7am-10pm, Thu 11am-10pm, Sat-Sun 8.30am-7.30pm
www.heidelberger-stadtwerke.de

Indoor swimming pool with a sauna in the Sportzentrum Ziegelhausen, which has a warm bathing day twice a week with 30° C water temperature.

● **Q SPA**
In the Crowne Plaza Heidelberg City Centre Kurfürstenanlage 1 (Bergheim)
tel. 06221/917702
▲ Adenauerplatz, Poststraße
◆ 7am-11.30pm
www.ihg.com

An oasis of relaxation in Tuscan-style surroundings with Jacuzzi, sauna, steam bath, plunge pool and swimming pool, rest area and sun beds.

● **MASSAGE ROYAL**
Friedrich-Ebert-Anlage 12 (Bergheim)
tel. 06221/543368

▲ Adenauerplatz, Poststraße
◆ Tue-Fri 11am-7.30pm, Sat 10am-6.30pm
www.massagesalon heidelberg.de

With a whole-body massage with aromatic oils, an African baobab massage or a foot reflexology massage, you can definitely relax here.

● **PANORAMA SPA CLUB**
In the Europäischer Hof Friedrich-Ebert-Anlage 1
tel. 06221/5150
▲ Adenauerplatz, Poststraße
◆ Sun-Thu 9am-9pm, Fri 9am-10pm
www.europaeischerhof.com

A spa above the roofs of Heidelberg with a sauna, sanarium, steam bath, sun beds, outdoor terrace and state-of-the-art equipment for a workout.

● **SALZRAUM HEIDELBERG**
Rohrbacher Straße 20
(Weststadt)
tel. 06221/9148877
▲ Adenauerplatz,
Poststraße
◆ Mon-Fri 11am-7pm,
Sat noon-6pm
www.salzraum-heidelberg.de

The "salt room", which
consists entirely of natural
crystal salt, truly gives a
feeling of well-being, not
only for the respiratory
system and the skin. You
can also relax on the jade
massage beds.

● **ORCHID THAI-MASSAGE**
Bergheimer Straße 125
(Bergheim)
tel. 06221/161645
▲ Betriebshof
◆ 10am-10pm
www.orchid-heidelberg.com

An authentic Thai massage
to tone you up.

● **THERMALSCHWIMMBAD**
Vangerowstraße 4
tel. 06221/5132877
▲ Volkshochschule
◆ 8am-9pm
www.heidelberger-
stadtwerke.de

Thermal swimming pool
that gains particular
charm from the wonderful
view and the lovely loca-
tion beneath big old trees.

● **F&B REICH**
In the Marriott Hotel
Vangerowstraße 16
tel. 06221/169920
▲ Betriebshof
◆ Mon, Wed, Fri 9am-8pm,
Tue, Thu 9am-10pm,
Sat-Sun 9am-7pm
fitnessbeautyreich.eu

Here you can relax in
the spa zone with a view
of the Neckar, get fit on
the training equipment
in the gym area, or spoil
yourself with a massage or
cosmetic treatment.

BERGFRIEDHOF

For a walk or to meditate in peace, the
old cemetery called Bergfriedhof on the
site of a former vineyard on the border
between the Weststadt and Südstadt is
always worth visiting. When the garden
designer Johann Christian Metzger laid
out this non-denominational cemetery
in 1844, he planned to retain exist-
ing features of the topography and a
natural appearance of the site. Today
visitors can walk around an area of 17
hectares with a network of winding
paths totalling 23 kilometres and more
than 18 terraces among a rich variety
of vegetation, including ancient trees
and shrubs. The famous people who
are buried here include Friedrich Ebert
(German president during the Weimar

Republic), the composer and conductor
Wilhelm Furtwängler, the scientists Carl
Bosch and Robert Bunsen, and the poet
Hilde Domin.

Steigerweg 20,
▲ *West-/Südstadt, Bergfriedhof*

Culture

HEIDELBERGER FRÜHLING

Every year the international Heidelberger Frühling music festival in March and April stages approximately 100 events, inviting connoisseurs and newcomers alike to enter the world of classical music with world stars

and young artists. The Heidelberger Frühling is characterised by its aim to be a mediator of music, to get people to think about the impact of music on society and their own lives. For this reason the festival has a different overall motto each year, which is discussed more deeply in lectures, workshops and talks with artists, and thus enables the performers and the audiences to engage in an informal exchange of views. In addition to major concert evenings in festive surroundings, it is above all projects such as the string quartet festival and the Festival Academy that constitute the appeal of this event.

www.heidelberger-fruehling.de

MUSIC

● **COLLEGIUM MUSICUM**
Augustinergasse 7
(Old Town)
▲ Universitätsplatz
tel. 06221/542212
www.uni-heidelberg.de

As representatives of the quality of the university music, this orchestra and choir stage regular concerts and are a fixture in the musical life of Heidelberg.

● **KONGRESSHAUS STADTHALLE HEIDELBERG**
Neckarstaden 24
(Old Town)
▲ Kongresshaus
tel. 06221/5844444
www.heidelberg-kongresshaus.de

A great variety of performances are staged in the main auditorium: the programme ranges from classical concerts and pop or rock events to cabaret and comedy.

● **JAZZHAUS HEIDELBERG**
Leyergasse 6
tel. 06221/4332040
▲ Neckarmünz-Platz
www.jazzhaus-hd.de

In the vaults of the old cellar, some 150 concerts a year are held, with an emphasis on modern jazz, but also evenings of soul, blues, rhythm'n blues, rock and chansons.

● **PHILHARMONISCHES ORCHESTER HEIDELBERG**
Theaterstraße 10
(Old Town)
▲ Peterskirche, Universitätsplatz
Tickets and information:
tel. 06221/582000,
tickets@theater.heidelberg.de
www.theaterheidelberg.de

The general director of music, Elias Grandy, takes the opera and concert orchestra on a musical journey to all points of the compass, and presents internationally famous artists.

● **SINFONIEORCHESTER TONART**
Heinrich-Fuchs-Straße 22
tel. 06221/1878171
Programme:
www.tonart-heidelberg.de

This ensemble of students and amateurs with many years of experience plays varied programmes to a high standard under its conductor Knud Jansen.

THEATRE & CABARET

● **AHA-UNTERWEGS-THEATER**
HebelHalle/Hebelstraße 9 (Weststadt)
▲ Rudolf-Diesel-Straße
tel. 01517/5090421
www.art-ort.net

This company based in the HebelHalle moves between the genres of dance, acrobatics and drama, and aims to express itself in its own inimitable style.

● **ROADSIDE THEATER**
Kirchheimer Weg 4
▲ Rudolf-Diesel-Straße

tel. 06221/175020
www.roadsidetheater.com

The English-language programme of this stage for amateur performers of the US Army mainly revolves around dance and singing.

● **ROMANISCHER KELLER**
Seminarstraße 3 / corner of Kettengasse (Old Town)
▲ Universitätsplatz
tel. 06221/542769
theater.rs.uni-heidelberg.de

The university theatre, a forum for student drama and the independent theatre scene and venue for cabaret, music and culture.

THE STUDENT PRINCE

The play *Alt-Heidelberg*, based on a story by Wilhelm Meyer-Förster, premiered in Berlin in 1901 and made Heidelberg famous all over the world. Derided by Kurt Tucholsky as a soulful melodrama, in the first half of the 20th century it was among the most-performed plays and was filmed several times. The story of the heir to the throne Karl-Heinrich, a student in a Heidelberg fraternity who falls in love below his station with the pretty inn-keeper's daughter Kathie but has to sacrifice his love for raison d'état, was the model for the Broadway musical by Sigmund Romberg that was a smash hit from 1924 under the title *The Student Prince* and was often performed at the Heidelberger Schloss-festspiele.

Culture

HEIDELBERGER SCHLOSSFESTSPIELE

Could there be a more beautiful backdrop for plays than the world-famous ruined castle? If you would like to experience this for yourself, book tickets for the Schlossfestspiele (castle festival) in summer. Established in 1926 with a performance of *Midsummer Night's Dream*, the festival came to an end during the Weimar Republic and was not revived until 1974 with the old Heidelberg musical *The Student Prince*. Today it is run by Heidelberg's mu-

nicipal theatre, and puts on drama and opera in a variety of venues in the castle under Jürgen Popig as artistic director. Added to this is an exciting and diverse programme of concerts that encompasses lively hits from operetta, favourite Italian opera arias, classic music from the movies and summer concerts.

www.heidelberger-schlossfestspiele.de

● **TAETER-THEATER**
Bergheimer Straße 147
▲ Hauptbahnhof, Betriebshof
tel. 06221/163333
www.taeter-theater.de

The repertoire of this theatre, where director Wolfgang Graczol stages dramas in collaboration with amateur actors, ranges from classical to contemporary pieces.

● **THEATER UND ORCHESTER HEIDELBERG/ JUNGES THEATER**
Theaterstraße 10
(Old Town)
Tickets and information:
tel. 06221/582000;
tickets@theater. heidelberg.de
www.theaterheidelberg.de

A theatre with five fields of activity: opera, concerts, drama, dance, and children's and youth theatre in a newly renovated old theatre, in the Zwinger and at other venues. Under the direction of Holger Schultze its programme combines the traditional and the modern. Thanks to the Dance Company Nanine Linning/Theater Heidelberg, the Theater und Orchester Heidelberg now has its own dance ensemble again.

● **TIKK - THEATER IM KULTURHAUS KARLSTOR-BAHNHOF**
Am Karlstor 1 (Old Town)
▲ S-Bahnhof Altstadt
tel. 06221/978911
www.karlstorbahnhof.de

Whether theatre, dance, cabaret or readings, the stage of this arts centre has a wide-ranging programme covering different genres.

● **ZIMMERTHEATER HEIDELBERG**
Hauptstraße 118
(Old Town)
tel. 06221/21069
▲ Universitätsplatz
www.zimmertheaterhd.de

For more than 60 years this privately run theatre with just 93 seats in picturesque backyard premises has been presenting contemporary drama on a studio stage, including premieres of new works.

CINEMAS

● DIE KAMERA
Brückenstraße 26
(Neuenheim)
▲ Brückenstraße
tel. 06221/409802
www.gloria-kamera-kinos.de

Small arthouse cinema screening films out of the mainstream.

● GLORIA & GLORIETTE
Hauptstraße 146
(Old Town)
▲ Peterskirche,
Universitätsplatz
tel. 06221/25319

This arthouse cinema often shows films in the original language.

● KARLSTORKINO
Am Karlstor 1, (Old Town)
▲ S-Bahnhof Altstadt,
Heidelberg Altstadt
tel. 06221/978918
www.karlstorkino.de

An ambitious, non-commercial movie programme that aims to widen the horizons of its audience for films and film history.

● KINO IM MARSTALCAFÉ
Marstallhof 1 (Old Town)
▲ Kongresshaus
tel. 06221/542657
*www.studentenwerk.
uni-heidelberg.de*

Student atmosphere: comedies and movies for cinéastes, films that are high-brow and low-brow, moving and thrilling.

GALERIE EDITION STAECK

Among the many galleries in Heidelberg, the best-known is surely that of the graphic artist Klaus Staeck (born 1938), who since 1986 has been visiting professor at the Academy of Art in Düsseldorf and since 2006 president of the Academy of Arts in Berlin. Founded by Staeck in 1965 under the name Edition Tangente, it exhibits 20th-century works as well as postcards, posters, objects and books by the artist himself.

His satirical posters and classic works of political art, and his critical attitude to politics, have reached a wide audience through his mass sales of postcards.

Ingrimstraße 3
▲ Alte Brücke
www.edition-staeck.de

Museums

● ANTIKENMUSEUM UND ABGUSS-SAMMLUNG
➤ p. 22

● CARL BOSCH MUSEUM
Schloss-Wolfsbrunnen-weg 4
tel. 06221|603616
▲ Hausackerweg
◆ Fri-Wed 10am-5pm
www.carl-bosch-museum.de

Fascinating insights into the life and discoveries of the Nobel laureate Carl Bosch.

● DEUTSCHES APOTHEKENMUSEUM
➤ p. 32

● DOKUMENTATIONS-UND KULTURZEN-TRUM DEUTSCHER SINTI UND ROMA
Bremeneckgasse 2
tel. 06221/981102
▲ Rathaus/Bergbahn
◆ Tue 9.30am-6.45pm, Wed-Fri 9.30am-4.30pm, Sat-Sun 11am-4.30pm
www.sintiundroma.de

The most important place of memorial in Germany for the victims of the Porajmos, the persecution of Sinti and Roma by the Nazis.

HOMO HEIDELBERGENSIS

The collection of the Institute for Earth Science contains one of the most important finds in the history of humanity: the 600,000-year-old lower jaw of Homo heidelbergensis. "Heidelberg man" owes his name to the place where the find was made, in a sand pit near Mauer close to Heidelberg. In evolutionary terms Homo heidelbergensis developed from Homo erectus, and evolved further to become Neanderthal man about 200,000 years ago in Europe. From parts of skeletons that have been found it is known that Heidelberg man was a successful hunter in Europe and parts of Africa, living mainly by hunting big game.

Institut für Geowissenschaften, Im Neuenheimer Feld 234-236 (Neuenheim)
◆ Mon-Fri 9am-5pm, www.geow.uni-heidelberg.de

● HEIDELBERGER KUNSTVEREIN
Hauptstraße 97 (Old Town)
tel. 06221/184086
▲ Peterskirche
◆ Tue, Wed, Fri noon-7pm, Thu 3-10pm, Sat-Sun 11am-7pm
www.hdkv.de

Contemporary art in a large bright gallery on three floors.

● KARTONMODELL-MUSEUM
Karlsruher Straße 76-78 (Rohrbach)
tel. 06221/7353560
▲ Rohrbach/Markt
◆ Tue+Thu 5pm-8pm, Sat+Sun 10am-1pm
www.ifkca-institut.de

Five centuries of cardboard models.

● KURPFÄLZISCHES MUSEUM
➤ p. 45 ff.

● MUSEUM HAUS CAJETH
Haspelgasse 12 (Old Town)
tel. 06221/24466
▲ Marstallstraße
◆ Mon-Sat 11am-5pm
www.cajeth.de

Museum with paintings by unknown artists.

● **SAMMLUNG DES ÄGYPTOLOGISCHEN INSTITUTS**
Marstallhof 6
(1st floor/Old Town)
tel. 06221/542536
▲ Marstallstraße
◆ on request
www.uni-heidelberg.de

The collection of the institute for Egyptology explains the life of the ancient Egyptians and their religious beliefs.

● **STIFTUNG REICHSPRÄSIDENT-FRIEDRICH-EBERT-GEDENKSTÄTTE**
➤ p. 15

● **STUHLMUSEUM**
Plöck 16 (Old Town)
tel. 06221/149874
▲ Bismarckplatz
◆ Mon-Fri 9am-noon, 1-3.30pm
www.stadtmission-hd.de

The chair museum illuminates the subject of seating.

● **TEXTILSAMMLUNG MAX BERK/KUR-PFÄLZISCHES MUSEUM**
Brahmsstraße 8
(Ziegelhausen)
tel. 06221/800317
▲ Brahmsstraße
◆ Wed, Sat-Sun 1-6pm
www.museum-heidelberg.de

In addition to a collection of women's fashion and production machinery this museum explains production methods and the use of various kinds of animal and plant fibres in textiles.

● **VÖLKERKUNDE-MUSEUM**
Hauptstraße 235
(Palais Weimar)
tel. 06221/22067
▲ Neckarmünzplatz, Altstadt rail station
◆ Wed-Sat 2-6pm, Sun 11am-6pm
www.voelkerkunde museum-vpst.de

Works of art and ethno-graphic items from Asia, Africa and Oceania, as well as changing exhibitions about the art and culture of various regions.

SAMMLUNG PRINZHORN

To collect works produced in psychiatric clinics was a most extraordinary idea in the early 20th century. Because the doctor and art historian Hans Prinzhorn hoped to be able to use the paintings for diagnosis and to find an elementary, undistorted way of accessing art, he collected the works of his psychiatric patients and published them in 1922 in *Artistry of the Mentally Ill*. In his life-time the medical profession rejected his ideas, but today Prinzhorn is regarded as a pioneer of this interdisciplinary approach. Artists such as Paul Klee, Max Ernst and Pablo Picasso were fascinated and inspired by these "works of madness". The power and beauty of the pictures can be appreciated today in the lecture-theatre building of what was once the neurological clinic, where parts of the collection, which now consists of 5,000 works, are on show in changing exhibitions.

Psychiatrische Universitätsklinik
Voßstraße 4 (Bergheim)
▲ *Thibautstraße*
◆ *Opening times during exhibitions:*
Tue, Thu-Sun 11am-5pm, Wed 11am-8pm
www.prinzhorn.ukl-hd.de

Shopping

A STUDENT KISS FROM HEIDELBERG

Once you have tried this delicious confection made from chocolate, nougat and waffle, you will not want to live without it. This must have been the sentiment of the young ladies who liked to meet in Café Knösel in the second half of the 19th century. As they were only allowed to go there accompanied by eagle-eyed governesses, the students who were present could do no more than cast hopeful glances at them. This gave the humorous chocolatier and pastry cook Fridolin Knösel the brilliant idea of creating an especially exquisite chocolate treat, which could be presented under the name "student kiss" as a token of admiration without arousing the disapproval of the governesses. Knösel's student kiss has now become the city's sweet emblem.

● **FARBENREICH**
Plöck 75 (Old Town)
▲ Peterskirche
◆ Mon-Fri 11am-7pm, Sat 11am-4pm
www.farbenreich-shop.de

Fabrics and wallpaper in retro design, modern jewellery, bags, crockery, cards, baskets, boxes and knick-knacks – here you can rummage through lots of colourful items.

● **HEIDELBERGER ZUCKERLADEN**
Plöck 52 (Old Town)
▲ Peterskirche
◆ Tue-Fri noon-7pm, Sat 11am-5pm
www.zuckerladen.de

If you have a sweet tooth, this place is heaven. Everything from lollipops, nougat and marzipan to wine gums, all in old-fashioned jars.

● **HOLGERSONS**
Theaterstraße 2 a (Old Town)
▲ Kongresshaus
◆ Mon-Fri 10am-6.30pm, Sat 10.30am-6pm
www.holgersons.de

Come here to buy things of beauty for everyday use, or to drink a cup of coffee in the sunshine.

● **L'EPICERIE – MAGALI SOULIE**
Hauptstraße 35 (backyard/Old Town)
▲ Bismarckplatz
◆ Mon 1-7pm, Tue-Fri 11am-7pm, Sat 10am-6pm
www.lepicerie.de

If you would like to pick up oil, vinegar, spices or unusual flavours of chocolate, the selection here is wide.

● **MUSIKZIMMER HEIDELBERG**
Untere Straße 10 (Old Town)
▲ Marstallstraße
◆ Mon-Sat noon-7pm
www.facebook.com/ musikzimmer.heidelberg

A small store with a big selection, especially vinyl.

● **PRALINENMANU-FAKTUR VORBACH HEIDELBERG**
Hauptstraße 211
(Old Town)
▲ Rathaus/Bergbahn
◆ Tue-Sat 11am-5pm
www.vorbachpralinen.com

This manufactory of fine chocolates sells truffles with names like "Heidelberg love story" and "castle mixture". Just the place for self-indulgence.

● **ROOM MATE**
Plöck 20 (Old Town)
▲ Adenauerplatz
◆ Di-Fr 11am-2pm, 3-7pm, Sat 11am-6.30pm
www.room-mate.biz

If you are looking around for attractive items for the home, you will find something here.

● **SPIEL & SACHEN**
Brückenstraße 34
(Neuenheim)
▲ Rudolph-Diesel-Straße
◆ Tue-Fri 11am-6pm, Sat 10am-1pm
www.spiel-sachen-hd.de

Come here to find toys for younger and older kids.

● **UNISHOP**
Augustinergasse 2
(Old Town)
▲ Universitätsplatz
◆ 10am-6pm (Apr-Oct), Mon-Sat 10am-4pm (Nov-Mar)
www.unishop.uni-hd.de

Not only for students: here you will find gifts as well as lots of useful products for student life, all of it bearing the logo of the university.

● **WEINHAUS C. FEHSER OHG**
Friedrich-Ebert-Anlage 26
(Old Town)
▲ Friedrich-Ebert-Platz
◆ Mon-Fri 9am-7pm, Sat 9am-6pm
www.weinversand-fehser.de

Traditional family company that stocks a big range of international wines and spirits.

WINE FROM HEIDELBERG

Not only the wine villages on the Bergstraße route, known as the "German Riviera" thanks to its mild climate, produce top wines. As the famous giant barrel in Heidelberg Castle shows, wine has been made in this area for a long time. The district of Rohrbach is thought to be one of the oldest wine villages, as it is mentioned in a charter of Lorsch monastery dating from 766 in connection with the donation of a vineyard. Due to the outstanding conditions for making wine in this small but superb wine region, for example Heidelberger Dachsbuckel with its Riesling vines, Heidelberger Dornenacker, Heidelberger Herrenberg and Heidelberger Sonnenseite ob der Bruck, a vineyard opposite the castle at the foot of Philosophenweg, various sites regularly produce vintages that win major awards.

Addresses

EUROPEAN MOLECULAR BIOLOGY LABORATORY (EMBL)

The European Laboratory for Molecular Biology, which has its headquarters in Heidelberg, is one of the world's best-known research labs. It focusses on basic research in molecular biology, the development and transfer of new technologies, and training and services for scientists from all over the world. This research

institute is operated by 20 European states, with Australia as an associate member. The EMBL has outposts in Cambridge, Grenoble, Hamburg and Rome. Some 85 independent research groups work at the EMBL on subjects covering the whole range of molecular biology.

www.embl.de

● **HEIDELBERG MARKETING GMBH**
Ziegelhäuser Landstraße 3
69120 Heidelberg
tel. 06221/5840200
www.heidelberg-marketing.de

● **TOURIST INFORMATION AT THE MAIN RAIL STATION**
Willy-Brandt-Platz 1
tel. 06221/5844444
◆ Mon-Sat 9am-7pm,
Sun 10am-6pm (Apr-Oct),
Mon-Sat 9am-6pm
(Nov-Mar)

● **TOURIST INFORMATION AT THE CITY HALL (RATHAUS)**
Marktplatz
◆ Mon-Fri 8am-5pm

GETTING THERE AND AWAY

BY CAR: The Rhine-Neckar region is served by autobahn A5 and autobahn A6. There are direct exits to Heidelberg from the A5 and the A656.

BY RAIL: Heidelberg is linked to the ICE and IC/EC networks of Deutsche Bahn and has local connections (S-Bahn trains) run by the regional transport authority Verkehrsverbund Rhein-Neckar
www.vrn.de

BY AIR: City Airport Mannheim, approx. 15 km away, is connected with Heidelberg via tram line no. 5
www.flugplatz-mannheim.de

Frankfurt Airport is approx. 80 km away
(*www.frankfurt-airport.de*).
Connections from there to hotels via the TLS Shuttle Service Frankfurt:
tel. 06221/770077,
www.tls-heidelberg.de
Baden-Airpark, the airport for Karlsruhe/Baden-Baden, is approx. 90 km from Heidelberg
(*www.baden-airpark.de*)
and is reached via the Baden-Airpark-Express Shuttlebus from Heidelberg railway station.
The distance to **Stuttgart Airport** (*www.flughafen-stuttgart.de*), about
120 km, can be covered in some 50 minutes by the S-Bahn train service.
From **Frankfurt Hahn Airport** (approx. 150 km from Heidelberg) the Hahn Express Shuttlebus goes to the railway station:
www.holger-tours.de

● **HEIDELBERG MAIN STATION**
Willy-Brandt-Platz 5
69115 Heidelberg
tel.: 0800/1507090
www.bahnhof.de
◆ DDB Reisezentrum
(travel centre) in the main station: Mon-Fri 7am-8pm,
Sat-Sun 9am-7pm
Buses and trams stop in front of the main railway station.
Taxis wait at the first exit (east exit) on the right (between the tobacconist and the newsagent).

CAR HIRE: Europcar, DB Reisezentrum, tel. 06221/53990, Hertz tel. 06221/23434

BICYCLES: Call a Bike in front of the station (*www.callabike.de*), Bike on the platform at right angles to platform 1b, tel. 06221/8937345, *www.fahrrad-heidelberg.de*, ◆ Mon+Fri 7am-6pm, Tue-Thu 10am-6pm

BANKS

● REISEBANK
Heidelberg main rail station, tel. 06221/27872, ◆ Mon-Fri 7.30am-7pm, Sat 9am-5pm, Sun 9am-1pm

HEIDELBERGCARD

The HeidelbergCARD is valid according to preference for 1, 2 or 4 days, or as a family ticket for two days. It gives you free rides on public transport, admission to the castle including the trip there and back by funicular railway, and reduced prices for guided walks, tours, museums and exhibitions, admission to cultural and leisure facilities, restaurants and shops. The HeidelbergCARD can

be purchased in the tourist information centres at the main railway station and in the city hall, at Touristservice Neckarmünzplatz, in the Kurpfälzisches Museum and in many of Heidelberg's hotels.

BOX OFFICE

● KULTURHAUS KARLSTORBAHNHOF
Am Karlstor 1
tel. 06221/978911, *www.karlstorbahnhof.de*

● THEATERKASSE
Theaterstraße 10
tel. 06221/5820000, *www.theaterheidelberg.de*

MEDIA

PRINT: Rhein-Neckar-Zeitung, Wochenkurier
TV AND RADIO: Südwestrundfunk, Campusradio Rhein-Neckar, Rhein-Neckar Fernsehen

EMERGENCY

Police: tel. 110
Fire brigade: tel. 112
Ambulance: tel. 19 222 (from mobile phone dial 06221 first)
Emergency doctor: tel. 06221/19292
Private emergency doctor: tel. 01805/304505

Emergency dentist: tel. 06221/3544917
Emergency pharmacy: tel. 01805/002963
ADAC breakdown service: tel. 01802/222222
Lost and found: tel. 06221/653797
Help line: tel. 0800/1110111

PUBLIC TRANSPORT

● RHEIN-NECKAR-VERKEHR GMBH (RNV)
Sales office in main station
Kurfürstenanlage 62
Service number: 01805-8764636
www.rnv-online.de

Up-to-date information is available via the *rnv Start. Info-App* for iPhone and Android.

CITY TOURS

Tours organised by Heidelberg Marketing: tel. 06221/5840223, *www.heidelberg-marketing.de* Walk through the Old Town (Altstadt), daily 10:30am, also Fri 6pm, Sat 2.30pm in German, Thu-Sat 10.30 am in English (Apr-Oct), Fri 2.30pm, Sat 10.30am in German (Nov-Mar). Meeting place: Marktplatz, main entrance to the city hall.

TAXI

● TAXIZENTRALE
tel. 06221/302030

● TAXI DIREKT
tel. 06221/739090

● HLS-HEIDELBERG LIMOUSINEN SERVICE
tel. 06221/3893999

Heidelberg's History

Around 450 BC Celts settle on the Heiligenberg.

80 AD The Romans build a bridge across the Rhine.

1196 First written mention of Heidelberg.

1303 First evidence of a castle.

1386 Prince Elector Ruprecht I founds the university, the third in the Holy Roman Empire after those in Prague and Vienna.

1392 Prince Elector Ruprecht II extends the town to the west.

1400-1410 Prince Elector Ruprecht III, in his capacity as Ruprecht I, King of the Germans, founds the Church of the Holy Spirit as a burial church for the electors.

1518 Martin Luther's Heidelberg Disputation.

1556 Prince Elector Ottheinrich introduces the Reformation to the Electoral Palatinate.

1563 Publication of the Heidelberg Catechism makes the town a bastion of Calvinism.

1613 Prince Elector Friedrich V marries Elizabeth Stuart, daughter of James I of England.

1622 After the capture of Heidelberg by the forces of the Catholic League under General Tilly, the Bibliotheca Palatina is taken to the Vatican.

1689 und 1693 The town and castle are destroyed by French troops during the War of the Palatinate Succession.

1703 Completion of the town hall.

1720 Prince Elector Carl Philipp moves his residence to Mannheim, the new capital of the Palatinate.

1788 A stone bridge, the Alte Brücke, is built by Prince Elector Carl Theodor.

1803 Heidelberg is incorporated in Baden. In the reign of Karl-Friedrich the university is renamed Ruperto Carola.

1871 Friedrich Ebert, later the first president of the German Reich, is born in Heidelberg.

1903 The physician Vinzenz Czerny founds an institute for experimental research into cancer, the forerunner of the German Cancer Research Center.

1907 The lower jaw of "Homo heidelbergensis" is discovered in Mauer.

1930 Foundation of the New University.

1945 Heidelberg, largely undamaged by the war, is occupied by American military forces and is later the headquarters of the US Army and NATO.

1964 Foundation of the German Cancer Research Center.

1967 The Max Planck Institute for Astronomy (MPIA) is founded on the Königstuhl.

2000 Opening of the Print-Media-Akademie of Heidelberger Druckmaschinen AG.

2007 Heidelberg University is officially awarded the title of elite university by the German federal government.

2012 The first residents move into the new district of Bahnstadt.

2013 The US Army has vacated all of its bases in Heidelberg.

2014 Stefan W. Hell, a professor at the University of Heidelberg, receives the Nobel Prize in Chemistry.

2019 the first company moves to the Heidelberg Innovation Park, the ideas quarter for the digital world.

Picture Credits:
All photos BKB Verlag except Artshop U3-4, 8, 29, 43, BHP Agentur für Bild und Konzept GmbH 50 be., Chocolaterie St. Anna No 1 39 be., 70 ab.l., DKFZ/Tobias Schwerdt 21 Mi., EMBL 68, Galerie Edition Staeck 63 Mi., Heidelberger Zuckerladen 49, Heidelberg Marketing GmbH 16 be., 32 be., 55 be., 62 ab., Mi., U8, Heidelberg Suites Boutique Hotel 50 ab., Internationales Musikfestival Heidelberger Frühling gGmbH/Sven Hoppe 60 l., Institut für Geowissenschaften 64 ab., Jazzhaus Heidelberg 25 be., 61 be., Landesmedienzentrum Ba.-Wü. U1 ab., 44 ab.l., 71 ab.l., Leanders Leseladen 66 Mi., Print Media Gaststätten GmbH 23, 56-57 ab., Spanisches Restaurant La Tapa 54 be., Staatliche Schlösser und Gärten Ba.-Wü. 27, Stiftung Reichspräsident-Friedrich-Ebert-Gedenkstätte.de 15 Mi.,Textilsammlung Max Berk, Kurpfälzisches Museum 65 ab., Theater und Orchester Heidelberg/Florian Merdes 60-61 o, Theater und Orchester Heidelberg/Kalle Kuikkaniemi 62-63 be., Universität Heidelberg - Kommunikation und Marketing 17, 18 ab., 20 be., Vinyl Only 67 be., Zoo Heidelberg 46 ab.